Social Media Marketing 2019

How Small Businesses can Gain 1000's of New Followers, Leads and Customers using Advertising and Marketing on Facebook, Instagram, YouTube and More

By Gary Clyne

Table of Contents

Part I

Chapter 01: Introduction

Last weekend two of my best friends and I decided a boys night out was overdue. Ever since they got into the corporate world and I ventured out into entrepreneurship, we don't get to hang out as much. A nice dinner and a little party time would be a great way to catch up and unwind after the week I'd had, I thought.

Unfortunately, none of us remembered to make any dinner reservations beforehand so when the weekend arrived, we realized we needed to improvise. Saturday night dinner with no prior reservations in my city means you take what you get! Most of the "cool" eating spots are usually booked out days in advance. It's a small city, and there aren't that many exciting restaurants to satiate the demands of a millennial (I'm very picky for a guy), so unless you plan way ahead, you'll be stuck with the crappy places.

This Saturday night was no exception. We must have gone through six or seven restaurants all turning us down because they just couldn't accommodate a "walk-in" for three. Almost in despair and feeling quite irritated and hungry, we started making fun of the fact that McDonald's (a few blocks away) might be our best bet!

Paul came to a sudden halt and curiously stared at what seemed like a little old sign on a locked door that none of us had ever spotted before. He pointed sharply and asked, " Does that sign say restaurant entrance this way?"

We all moved closer to have a better look. With the dim lights, it was rather hard to see, but in our hunger fest, it was worth a look anyway. So we followed the sign to the side of this usually empty street and lo and behold, there stood a guy dressed in a waiter suite smoking a cigarette standing adjacent to a door, which had no name. We asked him if this was the entrance to a restaurant, and he nodded casually, took one last puff of his dying cigarette and said: "follow me." Down we went through a small corridor in this mystery room, and all I kept thinking was, "are we sure about this?"

That was the night we discovered a well-kept dining secret in our town. Once inside, the place was well lit, the service was excellent, the food was great, but it was mostly empty! No doubt why. One older couple sat on one side of the room, a young couple with a small child on the other, and us.

People just didn't know about this place. The restaurant was a year old, and yet even I never realized that building had a restaurant on the corner of the ground floor. Seeing as it was a boys night out, we spent the rest of the night talking about more meaningful things (like girls and really fast cars), but the thought still lingered in the back of my mind. How could it be that such a great restaurant had no patrons?

Of course, the owner wanted more business, but he clearly lacked the know-how of getting his restaurant in front of his ideal customers without overspending whatever little marketing budget he has. Sadly, he is not the only one stuck in this dilemma. Many small businesses are struggling to grow their brand awareness in today's marketplace. Traditional methods of advertising are usually too expensive for small businesses. Those that are somewhat affordable just aren't effective enough, and when it comes to digital marketing and social media, few have the right knowledge.

I'm sure you've come across such businesses in your town as well. Perhaps it's your business that's currently experiencing this lack of presence and absence of customers. If getting more customers is of paramount interest to you, this book will prove very valuable. Keep reading, take notes and implement immediately.

When you know you have a good mousetrap, should you just wait for people to show up?

Absolutely not!

And it is because of businesses such as that hidden restaurant from last weekend, and all the clients I've been working with recently that I've finally decided to put together this crash course for small business owners. I want to make sure every great business owner learns the best way to leverage our current digital and socially connected world.

What to expect:

This book will share high-value tips about Facebook, YouTube and other channels that you can leverage to increase your current audience reach and business revenue.

Secrets you'd never know otherwise unless someone generously shared with you shall be revealed throughout the subsequent chapters so make sure to go through them all. It will also break down the platforms into chapters with accompanying tips for both organic growth and paid advertising making it super easy to read and follow. It covers all of the essentials of social media marketing in 2019 in a practical way that you can actually apply to your business immediately so you can start making more money.

- How To Use This Book

Social media, in general, is a massive umbrella, which at times can feel overwhelming especially for small business owners who are either just starting out or lack sufficient time to be online. This book is here to act as a reference guide. Use it to your advantage and let it trim down the time and mistakes often accompanied with social media growth for businesses.

You don't need millions of followers or have a million dollar campaign to make effective use of social media and all it has to offer. In fact, everything I share in part II of this book is with the intent of showing you how to make your resources and budget no matter how small produce a high return on investment. Go through the mini exercises provided in the book, start crafting the social media strategy as I take you through it step by step and be sure to experiment immediately. Social media marketing, just like swimming, can only be mastered through experiential learning. I don't expect you to test everything at once. As you will discover in this book, I don't recommend trying to be everywhere at the same time. Start with one carefully chosen platform, give it everything you've got and generated a strong forward momentum before expanding to other platforms. How will you know which one to start with?

That is one of the answers I will be providing for you in just a little bit. For now, I need you battle ready, fully committed and prepared to win in social media marketing. I also require you to avoid certain self-destructive actions on social media. Let's tackle those first.

- Mistakes Small Business Owners Are Making

• Failing to establish the right metrics

A common issue with small business owners and the marketers helping them is a lack of clarity on how to effectively measure their social media efforts. Obviously, without a proper way of tracking and evaluating the effectiveness of your campaigns leads to wasted investment. This is something I dive more into as I help you build your content strategy so if thus far you haven't been able to measure the performance of your social media marketing, by the time you're done going through this book you'll have the right metrics and key performance indicators outlined so your next campaign won't be stagnant.

• Selling way too much

There's a reason it's called social media you know? Selling isn't the nature of social media; socializing is! Therefore, be very thoughtful and creative about your promotional efforts especially when doing organic social media marketing. I would go as far as saying that you should really avoid trying to sell things if you're doing organic social media marketing. Why? Because many users on social media come to play and connect on these networks not to be manipulated into hitting the "add to cart" button. Sproutsocial reported in 2016 that many people unfollow a brand on social media if it has too many promotional messages. Out of the survey conducted, 48% ranked this their number one reason.

In simple English - don't try too hard to sell your products and services on social media. Being overly promotional will create a backlash and harm your business long-term. If you want to be more direct with your selling, consider paid advertising. We'll talk about that in part II of this book.

• Spreading yourself too thin

Building a strong brand presence for your business will take time and effort. There's no shortcutting this. You have to put in the resources, enthusiasm and continually communicate informative, relevant messages to attract your tribe. It's hard enough to master one social network with all its nuances, preferences and audience behavior, let alone trying to take on three or twenty. Unless you have a big team helping you dominate the social networks, avoid making the mistake of trying to be like some of your social media gurus. Start small, be smart about your strategy and understand your ideal audience so that you can take it one platform at a time. Instead of being a mediocre brand that's everywhere, be a distinctive brand in your chosen platform.

- They Types Of Businesses That Need Social Media Marketing

I think this is something many small business owners struggle with. Let's think for a moment back to my story with the unknown Asian-fusion restaurant. The owner could easily argue his place isn't big enough to merit the need for an online presence or any social media marketing. Would he be right?

Think about your local bakery assuming you have one. That nice lady who is always talking to you like she's your grandma (and makes the best homemade bread ever) would probably laugh at the idea of being more active on social media. Is her business too tiny?

Most people assume marketing (any type of marketing) should only be for businesses of a certain size. I think that this isn't entirely accurate in 2019. Sure, traditional marketing was designed for big corporations and brands that can afford to write big checks. But in today's digital world where there are both free and paid opportunities to interact with fans and potential buyers, it's ridiculous to assume your business shouldn't be marketing. Social media is really valuable for all businesses regardless of size and industry. Leveraging social media to connect and build relationships with customers both existing and new does have a direct impact on your sales and bottom line. I don't know about you, but my business could always use more revenue.

In 2016, Michael A. Stelzner issued a Social Media Marketing Industry Report which revealed that 60% of participants strongly agreed that social media is vital to their business. And the best part about doing social media marketing right as a business is that it has nothing to do with how many followers you have. Instead, it's about building strong engagement with your audience and implementing everything I share in the next chapter.

Chapter 02: What Is Social Media Marketing Really?

I tried to find a formal answer to this question on Wikipedia and was somewhat disappointed. It says "social media marketing is the process of gaining website traffic or attention through social media sites."

How dull.

So instead, let me try to answer it based on my experience and current understanding. I see social media marketing as a continuous process of creating high-quality content that is tailor-made for a specific audience group on each of the individual social platforms with the intention of driving user sharing and engagement. Makes sense?

This goes without saying, but I'll say it anyway. Social media is the biggest trend in the history of mankind.

It has grown more rapidly than the Internet itself. Think about this simple fact... When the Internet was made publicly available in 1996, it took about ten years to gather roughly 1 Billion users. That means it reached nearly one in six people on the entire planet within the first ten years. I mean that's super fast.

But wait... there's a speedster!

On September 26th of 2006, Facebook opened up the possibility of having everyone sign up on their social platform. By Q2 of 2017, Facebook crossed 2 Billion monthly active users. That means reaching one in five people on the planet within nine years. That takes things to a whole new level. Facebook is quite literally taking over the world. Data from Statista shows every continent with human population is significantly active on Facebook with North America taking the lead with 62% of the people using the platform. If Facebook were a country of its own, it would be larger than any other country in the world and arguably the most connected one. That's just Facebook. I haven't even shared statistics from other platforms like YouTube etc.

The fact that we are so addicted to our mobile phones and the social media apps on them make this topic of social media all the more interesting for any small business owner because as you know, where attention goes, there's money to be made. Right now, all the focus has shifted from Television and Radio to social media. Which means if you're not using it already you either have to learn it now or lose a lot in the long run.

- The Past The Present The Future

I want to assume you're in business to make money, to make a difference in this world and to help people solve a particular problem. As such, it's time to start taking social media seriously. Marketing may have looked different in that past, but today and tomorrow being able to leverage the connectivity of our digital economy is the key to your marketing success. Plus it costs less.

In the past, traditional marketing was the only way for any business to become well known. If you wanted to acquire new customers and get the word out on your products and services, you needed to create announcements, business cards, brochures, direct mail, do TV and radio promotions and relied heavily on print advertisements in the daily newspapers, magazines, etc. Direct mail was a hot trend.

Let me ask you this.

How many times this week have you sat down at your favorite table in the morning with a cup of coffee and eagerly opening up hundreds of envelopes delivered by your mailman?

Most people would say, none.

How many times this week have you sat with a cup of coffee and gone through your emails, scrolled through one or two or three social media platforms, responded to a What's app message, etc.? Most people would say, multiple times daily.

The fact that you don't see this connection to your business growth means you need a mindset shift. The present-day marketing has been transformed by technology. Today, a business must include a website, social platforms, videos and so on, in their marketing plan. And as technology continues to advance, we can be sure the future of marketing will continue to shift and adapt as both human behavior and technology changes.

The great news about the ongoing changes in marketing is that social media and digital marketing as a whole has made it more affordable for all businesses (regardless of size) to market and advertise themselves. In the past, you needed lots of money to run advertisements in newspapers, Television, and radio. Today, it costs very little, and at times the only cost is time and sweat equity.

This isn't to say that traditional and digital marketing are at conflict with each other. As Gary Vaynerchuck likes to put it, both are important and can serve your business needs well. It all depends on your objectives. But there is no denying that at the present moment, most digital efforts will cost you significantly less than traditional marketing. And when it comes to tracking your ROI, traditional methods pretty much keep you in the dark. If we are to make an educated guess at the future of marketing, I'd say it's bound to be more of what we have today which is, more of a digital economy than anything else. We represent the new generation of marketers, and social media sits at the core of relevant marketing techniques.

So as you map out the next five years of your business, regardless of how you've done marketing in the past, I recommend integrating more of what's working rather than trying to stick to old, familiar and ineffective methods.

- The Difference Between Social Media Marketing And Social Media Advertising

The difference is relatively simple to understand. Social media marketing as I mentioned before is a continuous process where you provide value. The intention isn't to make a direct sale. It is to foster a relationship and encourage sharing and engagement. This ultimately leads to brand recognition, trust and finally a possible sale.

Social media advertising varies slightly in that; the intention from the get-go is to make an immediate sale. As such, social media advertising is offered by many platforms on the side because whether you realize it or not, even Twitter, Facebook, and Google are a business after all and companies need to make money.

To open an account on Facebook or YouTube for your business is free. Posting valuable content and organically growing your audience is also free. But if you want to advertise and show up on the feeds of your targeted audience, that requires some money. By choosing to do social media advertising you enter into the "pay to play" league where the big brands are. At the moment, social media advertising is very underpriced (especially on platforms like Facebook Pinterest and Instagram), but something tells me the big brands will eventually take over, and the cost will rise just like it did with Google Ads. But more on this later.

For now, I want you to have clarity on the difference between these two as it will inform the kind of social media strategy you will create in chapter three.

- Understanding Some Fundamentals

Before rolling up our sleeves to make a solid plan of how to make social media marketing work for you, there are a few things you need to know.

1. This will require a mindset shift.

Business owners and marketers really struggle to succeed in social media because they approach it with an outdated business mindset or the wrong attitude. Do a self-check before embarking on this adventure to make sure you are adequately prepared. What you've been doing so far won't take you to the next level. Something new must happen if you want better results. Your productivity and execution will be contingent on having the right mindset. Get your mind right!

2. You must have a proper plan and commit to executing it.

While it's easy to think that setting up your account, publishing a few posts and tracking your likes is all there is to social media marketing, this is far from true. If you want your efforts to translate into direct ROI, you need to have a proper plan and strategy in place; otherwise, you're just wasting time and effort.

3. It takes time.

Many business owners have a tough time understanding the nuances needed to execute effective social media campaigns, and they underestimate how much time it will actually take to get results. Don't be that naive. This will take time and isn't necessarily easy or even similar to the other marketing activities you've done in the past. If you're not willing to go the extra mile, experiment and keep at it until it yields, then you're probably not ready to take on this adventure of social media marketing.

4. Come from a place of giving and adding value first.

If you want to do well on social media and give your brand the chance to succeed long term, you must add value first to the market place. The more unknown your brand, the more you must generously give and prove to the people that you deserve their attention and trust. Social media marketing is a trust game. Gaining attention is just the first step, securing their trust is when the real fun begins for your business and the best way to attain that is through generosity. When people see your brand and immediately associate it with "great value" you've won no matter what your competitors are doing.

5. There will always be a shiny new tool to distract you, stay focused on your goals and stick to the principles.

New software tools, new social platforms, and shiny bells and whistles will keep popping up. That's the name of the game in the tech space. Don't fall for the shiny syndrome so many newbies struggle with, as it will derail your objectives. In fact, you might realize (after creating your strategy) that you only need a few things to get you going. Just get the tools that are absolutely essential to your strategy and stick to one system and technique until you see results. Then put blinders on to everything else. Most of the time social media gurus just repackage something old in a new way just to get more sales. The fact of the matter is, the principles of business success and marketing are still valid; we've just changed the platform and method. So learn and stick to best practices; leave everything else for those who can afford to waste resources.

6. Social media is about building relationships and representing yourself in the best way possible.

Remember my definition of social media marketing? Always keep that in mind whenever you create content or ads for your audience. Business is about relationships, especially in our modern world. Your audience whether they are existing customers or potential buyers want to feel a genuine connection with you and your business. They want to feel like they matter to you. Your biggest job on social media is to make sure that message comes across in all your communications. The more they see you making an effort to form real relationships, the easier it will be to earn their attention and trust.

7. Establish a narrative that people can relate to.

Today's world is all about storytelling. If the backbone of your marketing isn't storytelling, you will lose on social media. You need to create a brand script that clearly takes your audience on the journey of transformation that your business provides. There should also be stories about the success of your customers to help prospects experience what it's like to work with you without taking the risk of paying you first. If you equip yourself with the right storytelling toolbox, your marketing on social media will stand out and help connect you faster with the right people.

8. Understand the social media lingo:

The first time I played chess, one of the hardest things I struggled with was understanding what my opponent meant. They would use terms like "ranks" and "files' and letters of the alphabet which totally threw me off. Naturally, I lost miserably. Couldn't even last five minutes in the game. That's when I decided it was time for me to take some beginner lessons on Chess. If I wanted to play chess again, I needed to speak that coded language.

The same is true for social media marketing. There are many concepts and words to understand, and if you don't take the time to understand what the core ones mean, you might find yourself chasing after the wrong carrot with your KPIs. Make sure you learn the social media lingo and continue to upgrade your vocabulary as much as possible. To help you get started, here are a few social media terms you must know.

• Content: This is whatever you are publishing or posting on your platforms. It can be a photo on Instagram, a tweet, a Facebook status update, LinkedIn article and so on. There are many different forms of content that you need to create, and it's crucial you custom tailor your content to fit each platform.

• Context: This is perhaps even more important than the content itself. If you're a follower of Gary Vaynerchuck, then you know how much he emphasizes on creating context around your content. He said that if the content is king, then context is god. Here's what that means...

You can have a great joke but if you don't get the context right (like a funny cat joke on LinkedIn or a long blog article with a joke somewhere in between the 4,000 words), very few people will appreciate it. But if you put that same joke front and center on Twitter, that same joke might go viral. Get to understand and integrate context when doing your marketing.

• Hashtags (#): I'm sure you know what a hashtag is but are you using them purposefully? Twitter, Instagram Pinterest, and Facebook all use hashtags, and you need to make sure you only choose those that enable you to describe your content topic or get your post in front of a relevant audience. Hashtags are meant to help your content get discovered by the right people. It's a way of connecting your posts to other posts on the same subject or trending topic.

• Engagement: This is the general term used to imply that people are interacting with the content you produce. It includes likes, comments, recommendations, and shares. Any type of engagement is good, but the shares are the holy grail of engagement.

•Shares: The currency of the social media world can be summed up into one word - shares. Shares are what matters on social media. There are other things such as click-through rates and potential reach but, to be honest, shares are what tell you whether people actually care about what you have to say. Having people engage with your content is good, but getting them to share is great. The more people share, the more you know people love your brand and message.

• Impressions: This is a standard metric used to measure how many times your post has been shown in users' feed. You may count multiple impressions for a single user if they have looked at your post more than once. Each social network counts impressions differently.

• CTR: Clickthrough rate (CTR) is the percentage of people that see your post who click on it. What counts as a click and what counts as "seeing your post" will vary depending on the social network. For example, on Facebook, CTR is equal to (link clicks/post impressions) X 100%

• CPC: Cost per click (CPC) is a social media advertising metric that tells you how much you're paying for each click on your ad on average. For example, if your objective is driving traffic to a landing page or piece of content, a low CPC means you're getting more traffic at a lower price whereas a high CPC means you're paying a lot for traffic.

• CPM: Cost per mille (CPM) is another often-confusing social media advertising metric. It refers to how much you pay for every 1,000 impressions. Mille is a Latin word that means 1,000. Suppose your goal is to get your ad in front of as many eyes as possible to increase brand awareness, in this case, watching your CMP is essential. Just like CPC, your CPM will vary depending on audience and location targeting as well as the quality of your ad.

• KPI: Key performance indicator (KPI) is a metric you use to measure your progress toward the chosen business objectives. In social media marketing, KPIs are the most important statistics to track so you can see if you're meeting the goals of your social strategy. For example, if your primary objective on social is to raise brand awareness, post reach and ad recall lift need to be one of your KPIs.

• LTV: Lifetime value (LTV) is a marketing term that refers to the value you place on each of your customers. If you don't know what the LTV of your customer is, then you're flying blind, and it's tough to scale your business. To grow your business, you either need to increase the value of your existing customer or expand your entire customer base or both. Knowing your current LTV helps you know which option is best for you.

These are some of the essential things that must be considered before embarking on the adventure of using social media to grow your business and brand exponentially. Now that you have them in place, it's time to establish the plan.

Chapter 03: Social Media Marketing Strategy

Is a social media strategy important for your business?

Absolutely, yes!

Think of it this way - A strategy is where you're headed as a business. The "plan" is what will get you there. Without a plan, you won't get very far in the crowded world of social media. You also won't know which of your efforts are working well.

Now, if you're looking for some secret sauce that takes out all the work, you won't find that here. But here's what I can give you... A solid strategy that can help you build long term sustainable traffic for your business that will inevitably lead to positive ROI in the future without you having to worry about anything. Stick to the following plan, and you will succeed. I have a template that has been working really well for my clients and me. Feel free to borrow it and customize it to fit your business needs.

Step One: Our social media goals are:
A.
B.
C.

Step Two: Who is our ideal target audience?

a. Who are they? Do we know their job title, age, gender, salary, location, etc.?
b. What are they interested in that our business can provide? Is it educational content, entertainment, case studies, etc.?
c. Where do they hang out online? Are they mostly on Instagram, Facebook, Forums, etc.?
d. When do they look for the type of content we can provide? Is it during the week as they commute or at other times?
e. Why do they consume the content? Is because they want to improve their life? In what way?
f. How do they consume the content? Do they prefer podcasts, videos, blog posts, etc.?

Step Three: What are we going to share, on which platforms and what will be our themes?

We can have different themes on each platform. We just have to make sure they all align with the brand mission.

Step Four: When are we going to share?

This has to be based on research that has been conducted and what we know about our target audience.

That's a simple version of how you can get more strategic immediately. You can also use this template for the different platforms you want to dominate. For example, you could have one created only for Facebook and an entirely different one for LinkedIn. Sometimes separating them could actually make life easier for you and your marketing team. If you just needed something quick and straightforward to implement now, this is all you need. But of course you want the nitty-gritty, don't you? Well, you're in luck. Keep reading.

- Get into the mind of your ideal audience.

This is the foundation of a smart social media strategy. You must know who your target audience is and why they use social media. If you know who they are and why they are on social media, choosing a platform to dominate becomes easy. To do this, we need to know their demographics and psychographics.

Demographics will tell us "who" they are. This includes age, location, gender, religion, marital status, income, education level, etc. Remember to focus on the details that matter to your business. For example, if you are in the tech space unless your company is catering to only a specific religion, any religious affiliation is quite frankly irrelevant. If you already have traffic to your website, determining this information is easy. Just check your database and customer history. If however, you're just starting out, then a tool like Alexa can help you get started. You can also use simple tools like Xtensio.com to start documenting your persona/s.

Psychographics will tell us the "why." This becomes even more important when we are doing content planning and creation. The more we know what our audience cares about and why they use social media, the more we can create content that is relevant and relatable to them. To do this, you will need to have a better idea of your audiences' outlook on life. Such as how knowledgeable are they about your niche? What are the common questions they have about your niche? How do they like to learn? Why do they go on social media?

- Instead Of Chasing Follower Count, Do This

Chasing a huge audience could actually prevent you from attracting one. There's an innate desire for most social media marketers to have bigger and bigger audiences. Those who don't have a big following dream of having it, those who already have a big audience want it to get bigger. The only issue with this mindset is that it influences the decisions we make, the content we create and how we promote it.

The real quest should not be for a bigger audience but for a more engaged and loyal audience. Your business needs meaningful interactions with the right individuals. That has nothing to do with follower count.

Instead of wasting energy trying to figure out how to make your audience larger, why not ask a different question? For example, if your next 100 followers all became true fans and bought your product or service, would that make a huge difference in your current sales? I think it would.

In that case, wouldn't it be more productive to figure out a way of getting those 100 true fans rather than chasing after the next 100,000 followers?

What would you need to do differently to attract your next 100 true fans?

Most business owners assume they need tens or hundreds of thousands of followers to be successful. Out of that assumption, they work at reaching a broad audience because they are afraid of polarizing or excluding any potential fans. I learned from my mentor, this is the slow path to social media marketing success in 2019.

If you can switch your mindset and focus on just the next 100 true fans, your aim would be narrow, you'd focus more on a targeted group, and you would create very specific content that only serves a particular group.

Yes, only a few people would LOVE what you create in contrast to thousands making it easy for you to be the perfect choice for a chosen few instead of the masses.

Shifting your focus to only the next 100 true fans makes you more attentive to your fans; it enables you to gain lots of clarity on your messaging and dramatically increases your engagement rate. As your communication changes and you focus more on building meaningful two-way conversations (since it's just a small group) you certainly wouldn't care very much about vanity metrics, follower count or virality. But you would care a lot about the customer journey and their satisfaction.

It's easy to get caught up with the allure of having a large audience but the truth is, growing your business and making more money doesn't need thousands of followers.

Don't get me wrong; I'm not saying you shouldn't be aiming for thousands of followers on social media. The point I'm making is that narrowing your focus to just 100 new true fans will help you make the right decisions and approach your marketing efforts the right way. The more focused, authentic and valuable you are, the more attractive your brand will become to the right audience. In a world where every marketer only talks about growing your Instagram followers, it's worth taking a step back and questioning what matters most to you and your business.

- The Four Ways To Drive Traffic To Your Business Using Social Media

Driving traffic to your business through social media is smart, and every business owner should be doing this in some way shape or form. It's not rocket science, and there are only a handful of best practices when looking to drive more traffic to your business funnel. Let's take a look at four of these, shall we?

• Earned traffic

This can also be called organic traffic. Some people call it free, but I think they are wrong. There's no such thing as free when it comes to social media marketing. Organic traffic costs something. It takes time, sweat equity and a lot of patience. To me, that's an investment. By creating valuable content and consistently feeding the social media monster (that never gets full), you eventually earn the trust and attention of your audience, and they start taking action when you ask them to do something. The more you add value to people on social media through published content the easier it becomes for people to find you, get to know about your brand and click on your offer or whatever action you need them to take.

Is this simple? Absolutely. You can start immediately. Is it easy? Definitely not. You will need to put in a lot of time and effort to see the rewards of this method.

• Paid traffic

This is leveraging social media advertising. I'm talking about buying Google ads, Facebook ads and other "cost per click" strategies. It is the fastest way to grow your reach and get brand awareness. The cost, of course, is your money. The more money you put in (assuming you know what you're doing), the higher your chance of success with this method. When you can buy traffic, you can start scaling your business really fast.

• Recycling traffic

For example, someone signs up for your lead magnet on Instagram. You can keep sending them relevant offers and send them to a new article, video, webinar, to your Facebook closed group, etc. That way they get to experience different aspects of your brand and the various offerings that you have. So they come in through an email, but they end up following you on social media networks or becoming an engaged blog reader, etc.

• Borrowed traffic

This is leveraging someone else's audience. By getting something like a JV or affiliate set up, you can be able to direct traffic to your offer from an audience that isn't even yours. For example, you can structure a deal with someone who has an email list of 100,000 subscribers. This person can now expose your offer to their list which automatically gets you in front of an engaged audience. You can borrow for money or for free depending on the nature of your relationship.

- How the young and unemployed are cashing in riches with social media

Before we jump into the meat of this book and get super tactical, I want to share some stories that I hope can inspire you to keep working on your social media marketing game.

The young, the unemployed, the high school and college dropouts are today changing the game of success as they find ways to create lifestyles that are rich, fun and freedom based through social media. You can see some of these stories on most of the major social networks. We all know of someone like PiewDiePie (a top YouTuber) that presumably earned about $4 million in 2013 alone according to estimates by The Wall Street Journal. He is definitely among the top earners of social media, but many other young guys and girls have found success either as personal brands or agencies serving small businesses.

Take the story of Dan. A young 19-year-old high school dropout (yes you read that right - high school dropout) who was shunned by his friends and family for quitting school because he hated it. He couldn't stand one more day of being in a classroom with old smelly underpaid professors who were trying to convince him that school was his only shot at a good life. Dan had dreams of traveling the world and sharing the beautiful scenery with his growing Instagram fan club. And he'd been binge-watching YouTube videos instead of completing his homework where he learned that local businesses were paying people to run ads that generate new customers. So when he quit school, his days were entirely taken up convincing local business owners to give him a shot (for free) so he could prove to them that he knew how to play the paid ads game well. All self-taught by the way, this seventeen-year-old finally got one business to say yes. It was probably one of the happiest days of his life. Well, scratch that! Second happiest, because the happiest day came two years later when he showed his mom a check for $10,000 with his name on it.

Today, Dan is spending half the year back in Houston and the other half taking adventure trips across Southeast Asia. And he's become so wildly successful (the first person in his family to make six figures a year) that he now teaches other young people how to offer digital marketing services.

His story is quickly becoming a norm in our society as more and more Millenials strive to become the generation that revolutionizes how we approach work and creating success. This isn't to say that school has no meaning anymore. In fact, Dan wouldn't have been successful had he not studied Facebook and Google ads. What I am saying though is that even people who don't want to follow the beaten path now have a fighting chance to create successful lives. The younger generation has already spotted the trend, and many of them are making lots of business owners very happy. Whether you are looking to do social media marketing as your business or you want to use it in your business to drive more sales doesn't really matter. What matters is that you recognize the potential you have within reach to create a life and business you love. Now, let's tackle one platform at a time.

Part II

Chapter 04: How To Choose The Right Platform

It's important to keep reiterating that your social media marketing strategy needs to hold a long-term view. You need an overall strategy that covers every area of your business and oversees all your digital assets and then you need simpler templates that deal with specific platforms that matter to you. The more specific your strategy is, the easier it will be to execute, delegate and monitor.

You are investing resources, effort and time into growing your following as well as your business and doing so on social media regardless of the channel will require some patience and persistence.

That being said, I recommend you focus on one or two (maximum three) social media platforms to focus your efforts on. Too many businesses are trying to be on all social media platforms (there are 200+ social networks and counting). This is a bad idea because in an attempt to "not miss out on getting more traffic" they end up dissipating their resources. If you want social media success that turns into business sales, quality is more important than quality. You'll end up getting better results if you invest more time and effort in a few platforms.

The natural question then becomes, which platform should you choose?

There is no easy answer to this. The right answer is that you should invest all your time, effort and resources on the network that hosts your audience. In other words, figuring out where your ideal audience hangs out is what should direct your social media marketing efforts. Depending on the niche you serve, you might have several options like Facebook, Instagram, Pinterest, etc. But for specific niches, your best efforts might be spent being in just one or two channels such as LinkedIn and Twitter, or LinkedIn and Facebook.

Therefore the next thing to do as we go through mapping out your social media marketing strategy is to narrow down the networks based on what you know about your ideal audience.

- Knowing Your Ideal Audience is EVERYTHING.

Since this is not a beginner's lesson on social media or growing a business, I already assume you've identified your ideal persona/s. I also assume you've used free tools like Xtensio to document who your perfect customer is. That little document becomes very useful for us at this stage. Pull it out and let's keep refining it as we go through this next part.

• Start by identifying the ideal age group of your customer based on the data you've gathered through active customers or your audience insights on the social network you already have. If you have Facebook (a must for any business really), then you can just go to audience insight from your business page and determine the age group of your primary audience. Then you need to evaluate that information with the information we already know about some of the leading social networks.

For example:

Snapchat and Tumblr have a higher younger audience ranging between 18 years - 24 years. So if your customers are teens and young adults, those two would be great for you. But they certainly wouldn't work if you are selling a retirement product. See where I am going with this?

Statista.com shows that in 2019 global active users of Facebook are as follows: 11% females between 18 years - 24 years and 16% males for the same age group. The numbers increase between the age group of 25 years to 34 years with 13% female users and 19% male users. So again, if your business sells products or services for this age group, investing more of your resources on the platform is undoubtedly wise.

All you have to do is just Google whichever platform you're interested in to get the latest report because they do change fairly often. Let's do one more platform before moving on to the next step.

LinkedIn stats for 2019 show that 29% of 18-29-year-olds are actively using the platform. The number percentage increases to 33% for the next age group of 30 years - 49-year-olds.

With this little insight, you can go back to your ideal persona and plot out the most relevant social platforms they are most likely to hang out. But we don't just stop there. We need to dive even deeper because we know demographics don't really give us a full picture. This is where a simple hack that I learned from my mentor because valuable. What is the hack?

Spying on your competition using a tool called Ahrefs. This is a paid tool but definitely worth it. All you have to do is type in your competitors URL, and it will show you everything from the best performing content to the most popular social networks they are leveraging. And guess what? If they are getting some traction there, you are more likely to enjoy success there as well.

Once you have a precise match between the ideal audience persona you have and the most relevant platforms where they seem to be hanging out based on research and your competitor's social activities, you are ready to pick one or two channels to invest in fully. This is how you can confidently assume you're moving in the right direction with your social media marketing.

The next step is to add so much value on your chosen platform that it becomes impossible for your ideal customer to ignore you. How you create that value is shared in detail on the next chapter for each specific platform. This is because all too often, we generalize content creation on social media, which is a big mistake. Every platform is different, and certain nuances must be adhered to for each platform. That's why I want to make this book as useful as I can by sharing different content suggestions for each of the major networks. That's coming next. Before that, let's talk about the metrics and aesthetics of your social content.

- Social Media Design, Analysis And Management

Most humans by nature are very visual beings, which means your social media images are a vital part of your content success. I could go on and on about why you need to make sure your design is on point with your brand message and identity, but by now I'm sure you've heard this over and over again. So instead of telling you why you need great design, let me instead show you how to enhance your current design.

First, make sure the color options you choose to use are conveying emotions. The right kind of emotions that will lead them further into your funnel. What we want to tap into first are emotions, not logic. In case this idea is new to you, let me shed a little insight on why emotions sell.

If you ask any buyer how they came to a conclusion, they'd most likely say it was a "logical" decision. But as psychologists have told us, we can fool ourselves into thinking we're more logical than we actually are. Antonio Damasio, a professor of neuroscience at the University of Southern California even wrote a book arguing that emotion is a necessary ingredient to almost every decision we make. Check out his book *"Descartes Error"* if you want to dive deep into the psychology of decision-making. It will help you build better landing pages, offers, and ads that convert better. I digress now. Let's get back into why evoking emotions by using the right colors for your brand is a must.

The color must support the personality of your brand and set the mood (overall atmosphere) of your online presence. Here are some colors and the impact they have on your audience.

Red = Energy and Urgency

Orange = Aggressive

Yellow = Optimistic and youthful

Green = Wealth and relaxation

Blue = Trust and security

Pink = Romantic and feminine

Purple = Soothing and calm

Black = Powerful and sleek

Second. Pay close attention to the use of lines throughout your image creation. When dealing with lines (especially if creating your own images or using stock images) make sure you deliberately draw the reader's eyes where you want them to go with clarity. Aim to have a distinct logical path that the reader can follow along until they come to the point you intended.

Third. Add contrast with colors, shapes, and sizes, as these are what make your design "pop." But you must do it tastefully. You can add contrast with colors, shapes, and varying sizes or making certain elements bolder.

Fourth. Group similar items together to organize, de-clutter and create a feeling of harmony on your social feed. By connecting similar elements together in an image as well as on your feed, you'll be de-cluttering your design and avoid that "messy look.

Lastly, I recommend you always use the same set of fonts, colors, and logos. Repetition is how human beings learn. It's also how people will start to experience a feeling of consistency with your branding. Over time, if you continue to use the same fonts, colors, and logos your business brand will have a unique and instantly recognizable look. Think of Apple, Coca Cola, and Nike. These brands are so consistent with their fonts, colors, and logos that you can easily spot them anywhere. That's what you want for your business as well.

Let's talk about how you measure and manage all your social media marketing efforts.

I recommend you do ongoing analytics and campaign focused metrics. Ongoing analytics is something you will track over time, but campaign or event analytics have a clear beginning and end.

Now, before you get crazy about measuring every single tweet, Instagram photo and Facebook comment, let's first think about the goals that matter to you.

Answer this: What are you trying to accomplish or gain through these social channels? And out of the channels you post on, which ones are most relevant in helping you reach those goals?

Generate a list of what you're trying to achieve from your social media efforts as well as what you want your audience to do with the content you're pushing out. Do you want them to read, share, reply, click, purchase, and engage?

Here's an example template that I use with my clients. Feel free to borrow.
1. We want to spread awareness of our new product/service to our potential buyers.
2. We want to get to know our [enter your niche] community on [enter your chosen social network] as well as the influencers in that community.

Once you are clear about that, it's time to choose what you'll measure, monitor and analyze, so that your goals can match actual metrics and behaviors. For example, if you decided engagement is your primary objective, then what is the practical form of engagement you want to track? Is it shares, clicks, comments?

Again, here's how I've been doing it in my business and for my clients. Feel free to borrow this too!

• Measuring awareness - we use metrics like Volume, reach, exposure and amplification.

• Measuring engagement - we monitor comments, replies, retweets, shares, etc.

• Measuring traffic to your website - we track URL shares, clicks, and conversions.

• Measuring brand voice - we track our volume relative to our closest competitors to see how much of the overall conversation around our niche is about our brand.

• Measuring fans and brand advocates - we track contributors and influence.

After you have your metrics, it's time to find the tools that can help you capture these metrics on the relevant social network. In some cases, you don't even need to outsource tools because the social network might have everything you need to measure, monitor and analyze. Google, for example, has everything you need with their Webmaster tool. Facebook also provides many of the metrics you will need. However, in some cases, you might need to get some third party tools or even build your own using APIs.

As long as you're clear on what you want to measure, it shouldn't be a problem finding the right tools to help with your measuring and monitoring. Just make sure you plan ahead and set things up for tracking before the campaign begins. As with every proper research, analysis, and monitoring, you need to report your results. Use your initial findings to set a baseline or benchmark for future measurements and share these early figures with stakeholders in your business if any.

Among the questions you need to ask and answer yourself are how do your numbers compare to what you expected? And how do they compare to related products and campaigns? If you don't know what to include in your report, I suggest you start with benchmarks and visualizations of your data such as graphs.

Monitoring and measuring your social media activities is so crucial for your marketing as it helps you understand how your business is doing. Make sure you're using reliable and consistent analytics to help you track your success. Let's dive into each of the social channels that can help you increase audience reach and business revenue.

Chapter 05: Facebook

What type of small business will do well on this platform?

All small businesses should be actively engaging in this platform. Whether you sell knitting lessons, financial services, sports gear, honey, cleaning products, retirement services, and anything else you can think of, there's an audience for you on Facebook.

Facebook is the biggest social media platform out there. And it offers you as a business owner and marketer the most data and the most targeted ads. The level of specificity at which you can target an audience within Facebook ads manager is almost alarming. I mean, these guys know a lot about a lot of people. For example, you can target executives who play golf regularly aged between 45 - 54 and who also live in the Bay area. That's how granular you can get with your targeting.

Facebook also gives you a lot of freedom when it comes to content. You can use images, texts, videos, infographics, etc. They all work. What does matter though is that you integrate your content into the platform and make it as native as possible if you want to have maximum reach.

For example, instead of posting a YouTube link of your latest video, upload the video directly to Facebook's own platform and then publish it. If you have a giveaway, publish it as a tab inside your business fan page. What I have found is that it's better to get people to engage with your content without having to leave Facebook as much as possible. People trust Facebook, and it helps them earn your trust when you don't make them leave their comfort zone.

Facebook Live

Since its launch in April of 2016, Facebook Live has gained much popularity. Real, raw and uncut seems to be the way to go nowadays. That's what makes reality TV so successful and it's probably why Live Streaming does so well. (Who would have guessed?)

Facebook created Facebook Live so that everyday people, celebrities and businesses could have the ability to broadcast live video directly to their followers and friends right from their mobile phone or computer. It's a feature that allows real-time connections to happen making it more authentic than recorded videos.

This makes it such a powerful way for you to show your brand's personality in real time and in such a cost-effective way.
If you want Facebook live to work for you, there are a few things to keep in mind.

First, you need to be personable and authentic. Don't over think things and definitely don't try to memorize a perfect script. Part of the charm of FB live is the raw and real aspects of messing up that usually happen to us as humans. If you do mess up on a video, just keep going forward. Don't try to be perfect.

Second, Get audiences to participate. Encourage engagement as much as possible and let it be a dialogue (not a monologue) as you shoot your Facebook Live. Ask questions, get some feedback, acknowledge those that live with you and once the broadcast is done, be sure to answer any follow-up questions or comments.

Third, you need to have a structure or framework before starting your FB live especially if you will be doing a broadcast regularly. Create a simple framework to follow that helps you have meaningful, purposeful and action based content that helps your viewers come out of the Facebook Live feeling like you made their life better. Whenever possible summarize the content, you share and have a call to action at the end.

Lastly, always remember to measure and analyze your performance. Keep monitoring yourself to see where you need to improve as a presenter and also the performance of the posts once the Facebook Live is done. A neat trick to add here that can help you maximize your efforts with Facebook Live is to boost the posts that do well to reach a new audience that you can then apply retargeting marketing to drive them into your funnel. Promoting a Facebook Live usually costs much less than regular ads, and in so doing you could build a warm audience that quickly takes action when you do retarget them with an offer.

Facebook Stories

This is one of the latest features that Facebook has released. Similar to Instagram and Snapchat, it is a quick way of sharing visual content and telling your story without updating your status. These stories are short and temporary as they disappear after 24 hours. The feature is focused around Facebook's in-app camera, which allows you to overlay fun filters (similar to Snapchat). You can also add visual geolocation tags to your photos.

One of the benefits of using this feature in your business is that you have the option of sharing specific content with specific followers of your business page only. And of course, within 24 hours that content will be gone. This can be especially great to test out if you have a limited time offer!

Another great benefit is that you can actually have a bigger reach with your content when you use Facebook stories. This is because once you post a Facebook story; it appears on top of the feed of your follower ensuring they never miss it (unlike with regular posts where reach has almost gone down to zero). This ensures your followers never miss important updates and content.

Due to their humorous and fun nature, stories can help you humanize your brand and show people that you are trustworthy, reliable and friendly. And as we all know, the key to getting more business is to have more people know, like and trust you.

Business Manager

If you want to advertise on Facebook, you need to understand the Facebook Business Manager tool. This is the hub that helps you manage your advertisements, pages, and audience. To get started you'll have to create an account by clicking the "create account" in the top right-hand corner and then just follow the instructions on the screen.

Advertising options

With Facebook advertising, you can choose to target people based on their demographics, age group, interests, income, the type of device they use and so many other characteristics. Facebook allows you to practically put into action the carefully crafted audience persona that you've created. But before any of it can be of value to you, what you need is to determine the goal of your advertising campaign. What matters to you most at this moment? Do you want to drive conversions to a landing page? Do you want to drive traffic in general to your main website? Are you looking to promote your business page or get more engagement on a specific post? Perhaps you'll need more than one campaign depending on your goals. Facebook allows you to choose the most relevant campaign objective and then you can target exactly who you want to reach, including the devices you want to target and the networks you want your ads to show up on.

Another critical thing to mention about Facebook advertising here is that you can create various types of audiences including what is known as a lookalike audience.

What is a lookalike audience? That simply means an audience very similar to the one that you're already connected to. This can be your email list subscribers, customers who have purchased your product or service or other types of audiences you may have nurtured within the Facebook Platform. Since you are creating a similar audience to what you already have, the results should be amazing.

For example, suppose you have been growing your list over the last couple of years, and you have an active and responsive email community of 1000 subscribers. You can upload this as a file within the FB ads manager and create a lookalike audience of new people who have never heard of you but share similar characteristics to those who are already in your list. Thus expanding your reach with just the right audience. Now imagine how cool this would be if you have a healthy enough list of prospects or buyers that you can leverage to create a campaign for!

Your ability to grow your social media presence as well as increase sales dramatically increases when you start leveraging tactics such as these ones within Facebook.

- The best type of content to post on Facebook

Every platform has its own audience, and each audience has their own expectations for what they enjoy seeing and engaging with. Learning how to post content that works on Facebook can help you get more engagement.

Facebook does well with videos, FB live videos, blog posts, and curated content.

• Natively published videos and live videos.

The best goal you can have with this platform is to build your brand and engage fans. To reach this objective, videos and Facebook live works really well. Many small business owners and personal brands are realizing that video posts generate the highest average reach among all post types. Buzzsumo recently analyzed 68 million Facebook posts and found that videos have higher average engagement than images and links.

Creating how-to videos, summaries of your blog content and inspiring or motivational videos have shown to generate the most success across various niches.

• Blog posts articles and curated content.

As a business, you should already have a good blog from which you extract content to share on your business fan page. Aside from your own articles I also recommend curating high-quality content from third-party pages and sites. Posts that are both educational and entertaining do really well on Facebook and could help you grow your likes and follower count significantly.

If you're not sure where to start with curated content, I suggest using the Facebook feature called "Pages to Watch." Facebook has a tutorial on how you can use it, after which you can just share the content that most resonates with you.

- Tips For Organic Growth On Facebook

•Post content that is highly relevant and interesting to your ideal buyer as well as your general audience. You need to satisfy the needs of your paying and non-paying audience. Try not to focus solely on your business and instead provide valuable information that can help you build a stronger relationship with current and prospective clients.

• Use questions at the end of your posts as often as possible.

The more you can address your page visitors personally and engage them by posing a question, the likely they are to respond and engage with you. As much as possible, invite your audience into a conversation with you on every published post.

• Publish evergreen content. After all, content is the most powerful tool at your disposal. The more timeless your main content is, the more useful it becomes to your audience. Keep alerting your audience of the most relevant evergreen content you've created and even experiment with boosting and repurposing your evergreen in fresh and new ways.

• Curate other people's evergreen content. You can collect posts from across the Internet and share it with your network as long as you know it's valuable and relevant to them. Spend some time reviewing and analyzing several posts on the same topic, make sure it aligns with your themes and share it out. You can create Facebook posts that are curation type posts in the form of Q & A's, "How-To's," Interviews, Video tutorials, recipe posts, checklists, testimonials and so on depending on your niche market.

• Be visually appealing. Even though this isn't Instagram, you still need to captivate and inspire your audience through solid visuals. It's also essential to use the right tone, don't be too formal and overall just be a good human!

• Less is more. Only post when you actually have something important to say. Contrary to what you might have heard from gurus, posting 5 times a day might actually hurt your business brand (especially if you're just regurgitating stuff or being too self-promotional). A recent research study conducted by the University of Colorado Denver Business School said that the number 1 reason people dump their Facebook friends is that they get annoyed of useless posts constantly bombarding their feed. There is a lesson in this for all business owners. If people dump their friends, they'll certainly dump your brand if you overdo it too, so make sure each post is fantastic before hitting publish.

• Use contests creatively and sparingly.
This is often considered the bread and butter of business pages for many brands. People love being part of a contest if it's interesting, fun and exciting. I encourage you to use contests periodically but remember it needs to be something edgy that makes people want to engage.

• Use organic post targeting.

Did you know you could even target your organic posts? Most small business owners assume targeting is only for paid ads. They're wrong. Here's how to do this. Enable the targeting feature from your page settings. Choose the people you'd like to reach in the News Feed. Make sure you choose categories based on the data gathered from your audience insights. For example, You can use Facebook Audience Insights to find out the websites that are most liked by your visitors, list the top 4 and target fans that match at least one of your desired interests. Once this is done, you'll be able to see on Facebook if the organically targeted posts perform better. If they do, rinse and repeat.

• Determine the ideal timing and frequency for your posts.

I said posting too much would be detrimental to your brand, but so is posting too little. If you don't post frequently enough, you won't look as reliable or authentic as a brand. The best way to avoid doing too much or too little is by creating a simple social media editorial calendar so you can establish a schedule that works for you. You can even start planning for seasonal topics, trending subject matters, etc. if you create a social media editorial calendar. But don't set something rigid, use it to guide your publishing schedule but remember to keep checking to see if different times/days work better for your audience. By monitoring your Facebook insights over time, you'll be able to tell what works well for your audience. The suggested times that you can start experimenting with are 12 PM, 3PM and 7PM.

• Partner up with Facebook pages in your niche. Here's a great example to emulate. Websites like Huffington Post and Elite Daily both have over twenty million Facebook fans and share a similar audience. They usually share each other's blog posts regularly, which boosts post views for both parties. At the same time, they are able to provide great content they didn't even have to create. To me, this type of partnership is what small business owners need. It helps keep content fresh and relevant for your audience and gives you the chance to increase your likes and follower count. This is smart marketing if you ask me, and a great way to organically boost your social media presence.

- Tips For Paid Advertising Success On Facebook

• Add your Facebook Pixel everywhere! Whether you're running a campaign or not, make sure you've activated all relevant Facebook Pixels. Add a Pixel to your website, all your landing pages and anywhere else you need tracking. What is a Pixel? Well in case the term confuses you, this is a single snippet of code that's added to all your site's pages which then allows you to track conversion and attribute them back to your ads. You can track general traffic, product purchases, content download, etc. Make sure you add the right and relevant Pixels to all the pages you wish to monitor before advertising on Facebook.

• Next is to make sure you're using the right sizing and spec requirements for Facebook. Remember every platform is different so familiarize yourself with the various requirements of each platform before publishing your ad. On Facebook, here are a few things to know.

The best image ads are 1,200 by 628 Pixels with a Ratio of 1.91:1. The text is 90 characters maximum. The Headline is 25 characters, and Link description can take 30 characters.

Slideshow ads should be 1,080 by 1080 Pixels, and the Image or Video Ratio should be 1:1. The text is 90 characters maximum. The Headline is 40 characters, and Link description is 20 characters.

The best Video ads should be .mov or .mp4, and the Ratio should be 16:9 with a resolution of at least 720p. The File size should be 2.3 GB maximum. Thumbnail size is 1,200 by 675 pixels. The text is also 90 characters, and the headline is 25 characters with a link description of 30 characters.

The best Carousel ads should be 1,080 by 1,080 Pixels with an image/video ratio of 1:1. The text should be 90 characters. The headline should be 40 characters, and the link description should be no more than 20 characters. Stick to this basic guideline and your ad will display accurately.

• Labor over your ad copy. Don't just copy paste the content from your landing page or something you used on a previous campaign. Every new ad creative requires time, effort and a lot of reiteration. Draw inspiration from content you've created in the past but do your best to create something fresh and super relevant. Consider the specific audience you are targeting with the ad, the language, and tone they would resonate with. Think about the type of information they would find most appealing and craft from that perspective. Just as we do with headlines for regular blog content, you want to try different angles until you find something that feels right. Once you like it, get someone else's opinion before publishing the ad.

• Create Page Post Engagement Ads. This is very effective if your business page already has a significant amount of page likes and followers, but you're noticing that many of them aren't being reached. Facebook's organic reach is down so if you have 1000 page likes and you post something organically only about 200 or so of your followers will see that post. That's roughly a 20% reach, which is very low. That's where Page post engagement comes in. By setting up "Engagement" as your campaign objective, you can get more people within your audience to see, share, like and comment on your posts. You can also run engagement ads to a brand new targeted audience.

• Be engaging and relevant with your ads. That way your audience will be more engaged and inclined to take action, and you'll also score well with Facebook ads Relevance Score. This is Facebook's measure of the quality and engagement level of your ad. Measured from 1 - 10 (1 = poor and 10 = high) you obviously won't get as high scoring as possible. Facebook scores you after your ad is served more than 500 times. Of course, this isn't always an accurate analysis of how engaging your ad is because it's gauged based on what Facebook predicts will be your ad's engagement relative to your campaign objective and audience targeting. The more you can concentrate on being super relevant to your highly targeted audience and offer the right context with your content, the more you won't need to worry about this.

• Show off your products or services with Facebook Carousel Ads. These are tailor-made for displaying multiple parts of the same product in a single swipe-able ad. They work best for e-commerce products.
You can add up to ten images or videos with ten different CTAs in the same ad, and you can also link out to different landing pages.

• Use Facebook Video Ads. Any strong marketer in 2019 is leveraging this and with good reason; it works! The setup process is just as simple as setting up a regular image ad, but the engagement, cost per result and engagement rates are proving much better than traditional image ads.

•Use Facebook Lead Ads to drive conversions and bring people into your sales funnel. Note however that these are a mobile-only solution. Facebook created this feature to help shorten the cumbersome process of taking prospects out of the platform to a landing page. I have found them to be especially great for service-based businesses. You can acquire names, job titles, phone numbers, addresses, demographics and pretty much any information that can be used to market or remarket your products and services. There's also the increased "trust factor" because your user will experience the entire lead from within the Facebook app ensuring they feel safe and "at home." Use this tactic to generate high-quality leads and to collect information that can help you create custom and lookalike remarketing audiences.

• Master Facebook remarketing by getting to understand your custom audiences. There are currently five ways to remarket. You can use custom audiences to remarket either by adding a customer file (such as an email list), targeting people who have visited your website (website traffic), people who have launched or interacted with your app or game, people who have come to your store offline or other offline activities (as long as you have this information) and lastly you can create a list of people who engage with your content on Facebook or Instagram. With each of these options, you also have the option of layering specific demographic, behavioral or additional interest targeting to refine the audience even more. This becomes the crux of Facebook remarketing and the more you do it well (adhering to mandatory laws such as GDPR) the higher your ROI will be.

• Experiment with lookalike audiences as well. Facebook allows you to create a new audience segment based off a custom audience you already have. Suppose you sell women's shoes and have a list of purchased customers. When you upload that list, you naturally create a custom audience of buyers who obviously loved your product. Now you can create a lookalike audience and have an entirely new segment of people who haven't yet bought your product but are very similar to those who originally purchased from you. And you can also layer in specific interests and other demographics to make sure the new audience is a perfect match. Are you starting to see the power of advertising on Facebook?

If so, what are you waiting for? It's time to start experimenting and driving more prospects into your marketing funnel.

Chapter 06: Instagram:

Who is this platform great for?

Instagram is a fantastic opportunity for E-commerce businesses, coaches, consultants, artists, and any other business that's mainly in the fashion, beauty, sports, entertainment, hospitality and service industry.

The developers of Instagram app surely did everything right. They built an app and launched it at just the right time. Their initial success was entirely organic, did you know that? Within three months of launching it in the app store, they reached 1 million users! 24 months later, Facebook bought the app for 1 billion dollars. And the rest, as they say, is history! I find their story absolutely incredible and by far not ordinary. But there are many great lessons we can from their Instagram success as business owners, and we can certainly learn to leverage the platform to our advantage as many marketers have.

Out of all the major social networks, Instagram still has the highest engagement rate. And in the world of Instagram, it's always about pictures. The platform recently added videos, and Insta stories options but few accounts are doing it well and greatly succeeding; it's still mostly concentrated on Pictures.

- The best types of content to post on Instagram

If you want to grow your audience and drive traffic to your business quickly I would suggest experimenting with the following types of content:

Quotes:

Inspirational and motivational quotes are the most popular content types on Instagram. Integrating your brand with motivational quotes can be a great way to stand out and if you don't have much access to great quote images just create your own graphics using free tools like Adobe Spark and Canva.

Photos of items from luxury brands or if you sell physical products such as fashion or food, you can post high-resolution pictures of your product in various aesthetically pleasing settings. You can also post user-generated content. If you are going to use user-generated content be sure to ask for permission from the original poster before reposting. One last tactic I can share about photos is that you can take nice "behind the scenes" images and share them with your audience. This can be of a product you're working on, your staff, etc. Be creative about this and make sure the quality is always high.

Sparsely clothed beautiful women (no surprise there!) What can I say is, if you can pull off a Kardashian type of content, you'll probably get attention. Who would have guessed?

Instagram stories.

In other words, use storytelling for your marketing. Shoot these short videos and share announcements, news, updates, introduce an Instagram takeover guest, offer giveaways and discounts and other quick, valuable tips that are time sensitive yet still valuable to your audience.

Questions in text form to engage your followers.

Video content also works, but you need to make it short, attractive and highly valuable for your audience. Some influencers do this really well. For example, if you are in the food niche, you could shoot 15-second videos with a full recipe. Such videos can do really well and gather you thousands of views and lots of comments.

- Tips For Organic Growth On Instagram

• Fix your bio and add a relevant link. You need to have a compelling and high-quality profile. It must be attractive and informative so that your followers know who you are, what your business does and why they should follow you. I recommend making your business name the username. If you have a personal brand, then it should be your name.

• Decide on a theme (main topic and relevant subject matter that you will cover on your feed). It's essential to decide on the theme as well as the design (look and feel) of your feed so that the overall feed provides a memorable experience for first-time visitors. Having a distinct theme will also simplify your content creation, and your ideal audience will quickly identify with your page as soon as they come across it.

• Make sure you're using relevant hashtags. The right hashtags will continue to give your brand exposure and bring in more of the right people. Use branded hashtags (unique to your business) and community hashtags (hashtags used by people sharing the same message). Use the Instagram search function to find hashtags related to your industry or check what competitors and industry leaders are using.

• When seeking quotes to post on your Instagram, find the ones that support your brand mission and don't overdo it.

• Leverage Instagram stories and use them to promote a blog post, announce a limited time offer or new promotions, etc.

• Focus on quality over quantity and make sure every post is attractive because that's the first barrier for engagement. This is the lifeblood of your Instagram success so learn the techniques and tools that help you produce good-looking images. Also remember to use the captions section whether you're publishing a quote, image or video.

• Be super responsive to your followers and answer every comment. Yes, you read me right. Every single comment. Unless you're getting thousands every day, you can easily respond to everyone and you should. There's no point of doing social media marketing if you'll be one of those many businesses that post something and never respond to the community.

• Find ways to encourage more User-generated content. Creating contests and giveaways can be an excellent way for your business to start receiving some UGC opportunities. The more engaged your fans are, the more they will participate and happily advocate your products or services. This is the best type of marketing you can possibly do on Instagram for organic growth.

• Get more organized with your posts. Here's what I recommend... Create a folder for "Instagram Social Media" and within that folder create one folder for each theme (topic) that you will have. This can be Quotes, Events, Promotions, Blog posts, etc. Within each of these folders, you will create a folder that is called "Posted." Then head over to Canva or whatever software you use and create content for each theme. Label each piece of content with an acronym for the theme and the number of the post, i.e., FQ#1 - for the first post in the "Food Quotes" theme, and so on. Do this for all themes and add the content to its respective folder. Now head over to your editorial calendar with the specific theme and number of post. Once you post the content on Instagram, move it to the "posted" folder. You can follow this process for all your social media accounts, and in so doing, you'll be able to go back to your editorial calendar and see how long ago you posted the content then you can easily repost it by finding it on the "Posted" folder. Execution is everything when it comes to social media marketing success, and now I just showed you how to execute like a professional for your business account.

• Use influencer marketing. While this may cost money at times, it doesn't always have to and can organically grow your following and drive direct sales really fast. Influencer marketing is on the rise, and on Instagram especially you can find all types of influencers. Some will require payment to work with you, others are willing to partner up and trade in other ways depending on how you negotiate. Take some time to do your research on Influencer marketing and start reaching out to the ones that align most with your brand and the products or services you offer.

- Tips For Paid Advertising Success On Instagram

• Promote only the best
Many business owners make the common mistake of developing scripts and ad copy that they assume will have the most significant impact on their audience. If you want to succeed with Instagram ads, I don't recommend this approach. Instead, I want you to go over the wealth of content you already have. You know what your current audience appreciates and resonates with. Look back through the images and videos that sparked the most engagement from your audience and repurpose those posts as ads. This will get you a huge life in response from that new audience you're trying to reach. Since success isn't guaranteed with every campaign you launch, I recommend starting with something you already know your audience likes as it's likely going to boost your visibility the most.

• Use image carousels to tell a story. Using several images to tell a story about your offer is a great way to grab attention. Using a story, you can intrigue the audience and quickly give them a taste of what it's like to interact with your brand as well as the solutions you can offer. But if you are going to use this tactic, make sure it is story-based and well thought out. Don't just post product images or meaningless stock imagery that have no correlation. Use the photos to create an experience and make sure you evoke the desired emotion. Think about how you want to make people feel as a result of watching your ad.

• Make your ads blend in. If you make your ads look like ads, then you won't do very well with your Instagram ads. Your audience will respond better when the post seems like original content as opposed to blatant promotion. If you make people feel like you're continually trying to sell them something your brand and sales will suffer even if you are using paid ads.

• Use actual people or images that contain faces in your pictures and video ads. This is because faces get 38% more likes than other content types and since you're investing money on this post, make sure you set it up in a way that optimizes your chance of success.

• Create a theme for your promotion. Once the ad is live, make a few similar organic posts to create a smoother transition that interweaves both the ads and your organic content. That way when someone does end up on your feed, they will feel a sense of congruency and consistency with your message.

• Use Video. Even though images are the most popular, using video promotions can offer a high ROI. We already know video performs really well on Facebook and since it's also the owner of Instagram, it's worth experimenting with video ads on Instagram to see if your audience reacts. Please remember to use the right specifications, as Instagram videos need to be really short. If you want a quick way of generating videos that aren't promotional, consider turning your user-generated content into a video and telling a short story about your brand. Then add a call to action that brings people into a funnel where you can make them an offer and add more value.

• Use the call to action button. When you create an ad, you can include a call to action button near the image caption (bottom right of the image), which offers you several choices in the messaging. Choose the one most relevant to your campaign.

Chapter 07: LinkedIn

Who is this platform great for?

Well, if you sell cute puppy clothes or muffin recipes, this is probably not the best social network for you. But if you are in tech, finance, insurance or any other B2B or professional space, then this channel will definitely be worth your time.

LinkedIn is incredible especially if you're in the B2B (business to business) niche. It is considered the number one marketing channel for B2B marketers and makes up more than 50% of all social traffic to B2B websites and blogs. LinkedIn has some of the best traffic out there and can work wonders in helping you generate high quality leads organically and with paid ads.

Did you know LinkedIn is actually older than Facebook?

Reid Hoffman founded it in 2002, and it's accurate to say his platform has used the slow boat to China when it comes to growth. Insiders report that in the beginning growth was so slow, some days they got only 20 sign-ups. Of course, things have picked up a lot since and LinkedIn has over 476 million members. They may not have been viral in their popularity, but they definitely became profitable reasonably quickly, and in the end, Microsoft ended up buying them for a cool 26 billion dollars!

On LinkedIn, people are actively focused on one thing: business. It's a professional social network, and your cat videos and crazy Gifs or too much profanity will definitely not do very well. People on LinkedIn want to learn about what's new in their industry, where the best jobs are, who's hiring and firing as well as how to increase work performance.

LinkedIn Groups

These are communities of like-minded professionals that gather to explore and discuss topics of interest or establish their expertise. I recommend joining a group if you want to expand your network and grow your content marketing audience.

- The best types of content to post on LinkedIn

A common question that many business owners will have when it comes to LinkedIn is, "what do I post?" This is a professional social network, so you need to be more intentional and thoughtful about what you publish here. Cat pictures and pictures of what you had for lunch won't cut it here. So be careful not to harm your image on LinkedIn by publishing content you currently use on Facebook or Instagram. Here are my best performing content types so far.

• Industry trends.

LinkedIn is a professional social network. People are there for business, to find jobs, hire professionals and get informed about the latest trends in their industry. Assuming you know your target audience really well, you can post industry trends and news articles. They can be originally created by you or curated from reputable sources.

• How to articles.

These work really well on this platform. Think more along the lines of teaching someone how to do something or make something. Tips and hacks are also well received on the platform because people want to keep improving their game. I have found that most people on LinkedIn are generally interested in informative and educational content.

• Thought Leadership content.

LinkedIn has created a marketing guide where they recommend that content creators should focus on being helpful rather than salesy. I see many business owners doing this a lot on social media and yes I know it can be tempting to focus on more on telling your audience why they need your product or services, but trust me, this isn't the best approach. More often than not, you'll just seem salesy. LinkedIn also shared on the same guide that "publishing thought leadership content on your company page is one of the most powerful ways to grow your LinkedIn audience." They also took the liberty to share three types of thought leadership content, which they believe will serve your brand well on their platform.

Industry thought leadership: Your perspective on news and trends as it relates to your industry.

Organizational thought leadership: Embodied in the vision and ethos of your company.

Product thought leadership: Centered on being the best solution for your customers.

• Images with statistics

On LinkedIn, the more you can share stats and information that makes you appear more knowledgeable, the more people will love your brand. Consider taking "stand out" statistics either from your case studies or from reputable sources and showcase them with attractive social tiles as part of your social media marketing campaign.

• Image Quotes.

Use this sparingly and only when accompanied with text to give the image quote enough context. If it is a motivational image quote, make sure it is relevant to your audience.

• Video content.

Both images and videos perform really well on LinkedIn and tend to generate a higher comment rate. Since you can now upload videos natively into the platform, I recommend you combine YouTube videos as well as natively published videos. The LinkedIn marketing team reports that video is 5x more likely than other types of content to start a conversation among members.

Consider creating video case studies and short videos series for your brand. Keep the content valuable, concise and customer focused.

Always include some kind of call to action in all your videos to encourage more engagement and connection with your audience.

• Company milestones, celebrating company culture and business success.

When done right this can be a fantastic way to give people an insider look at your company, how you're growing and the way your runs. It also gives people a chance to understand your vision and mission. Celebrate diversity, big wins and openly show your gratitude for your followers, employees, and customers.

• Company events and an invitation to other exclusive events.

If you have an event that's happening online or offline and if you're sponsoring an event, you can post content that drives registration. Invite people to attend or sign up for your event and be sure to use appropriate imagery and text to give enough context and get people excited.

• Offer your free giveaways or eBooks.

If you have resources, an eBook or any other lead magnet, this can be creatively shared on LinkedIn through quotes, mini videos, etc. Even if it's a paid eBook, you can still promote it by offering a free chapter.

• Curated content.

Many blogs, magazines and newspaper sites constantly push out amazing content daily. With just a little effort you can have lots of great content to share with your followers that is both beneficial to them and your brand even though you didn't create it. Use tools like Buffer to help you find awesome content to curate for your industry.

- Tips For Organic Growth On LinkedIn

• Make an effort to fully complete your profile (and company page if possible). You've got to make it compelling, add advanced applications, and tell people who you are, what your brand is and how you can help people.

• Branch out and connect to everyone that you find interesting. Even people that aren't directly related to your niche. Go for people in your industry, leaders in other interesting industries and those in your local community. The more you connect with interesting people that you don't know, the more your opportunities are going to expand and grow.

• Appy some SEO on your LinkedIn profile and company page. Just as you would optimize your website with the right keywords to help you with Google rankings, choose relevant keywords that you wish to rank for within LinkedIn. People are always searching on the LinkedIn search bar for experts, thought leaders, freelancers, and consultants to hire to solve the problems in their business. So make sure you add specific keywords throughout your profile, and if you do this right, you'll notice your name will rank higher for that chosen keyword enabling you to drive more traffic to your profile and company page.

- Publish high-quality content on the LinkedIn publishing platform. LinkedIn algorithms have a bot evaluating all the content you produce and classifying it as either spam, low quality or clear. Therefore focus on quality instead of quantity.
- Create fresh content and updates. LinkedIn recommends posting at least once per weekday.

- Post more video content. LinkedIn is interested in promoting the use of videos at the moment so you'll notice your videos will get way more reach than other types of content. Just as I encouraged you with the other social networks, be sure to take advantage of the video trend and post videos frequently. You can either upload the video natively (there's a time limit on this) or share a YouTube link form your channel.

- Keep in touch with your most recent connections. Make sure you keep nurturing the new and high impact connections you're making on LinkedIn. Immediately reach out once they accept your request, endorse them, give recommendations where applicable and nurture that potential of having a mutually beneficial relationship.
- Leverage groups. It's a great way to connect with a like-minded professional in your niche market as well as prospects. Create conversations about what's happening in your industry or the world with people who can appreciate it the most and from there, nurture the relationship.

- Tips For Paid Advertising Success On LinkedIn

For you to fully understand the full power of LinkedIn when it comes to lead generation and sales, we must devote a little time talking about LinkedIn Premium.

LinkedIn premium is the paid version offered by the platform. Most people only talk about the free features of the network, and although it can be a great starting point, if you're really serious about growing your business on this social network, a LinkedIn premium is worth the investment. There are several different levels of premium depending on one's goals and business objectives.

The first option is the LinkedIn premium for general users. It starts at $24.95 per month. With this plan you get features such as InMail, you get to see more profiles when searching on the platform, and you also have access to premium search filters. There's also the ability to view expanded profiles on LinkedIn and so much more.

The second option is the LinkedIn premium for recruiters. It starts at $49.95 per month and includes features like talent finding filters, saved searches with alerts for new candidates who meet your criteria and so much more. If your business is recruitment, then this is definitely a powerful tool to have.

The third option is the LinkedIn Premium for Job seekers, which starts at $19.95 per month. As the name suggests, this one is more designed to help someone looking for a job. It includes the ability to zero in on $100K plus jobs with detailed salary information, access to the job seeker community, ability to move up to the top of the list as a featured applicant and so much more.

The fourth option is the LinkedIn premium for Sales professionals commonly referred to as the LinkedIn sales navigator. It starts at $19.95 per month as well. With this plan, you'll get a Lead Builder organizer, introductions to companies that you're targeting and so much more. As you can see, this option is excellent for someone specifically working in the B2B space dealing with sales and marketing.

If any of these options feel like they might work to help you connect with the right decision makers and bring in more sales, I recommend getting a free trial to test them out. Some of the advertising ideas I am sharing below might require a premium account feature, but for the most part, you can be able to test them out even if your regular free account.

• Use InMail to foster more personal relationships from individuals you want to connect with either in groups or direct search. InMail allows you to contact anyone on LinkedIn directly, and it's very effective. Reach out to desired prospects and influencers in your audience.

• When a published content gets lots of engagements, boost it with "Sponsored Content." This is one of the native advertising options on LinkedIn that allows you to promote your content directly on the LinkedIn feeds of the professionals you want to target.

• Experiment with other LinkedIn ads options. LinkedIn has text ads and sponsored InMail ads that can be really effective for high-quality lead generation. You can quickly get in front of all the right decision makers and dramatically increase your sales.

• Use LinkedIn's Matched Audiences tool to retarget the visitors that are already in your sales funnel. This simple hack enables you to retarget website visitors and even add email contacts to target with your LinkedIn ads.

• Get the Sales Solutions platform so you can seamlessly target, research and engage with new prospects. This is an entirely different service from the unpaid platform LinkedIn has to offer. It is more account-based marketing with heavy-duty research tools and lots of insights, which makes it a powerful and worthwhile tool for a savvy business owner.

• Monitor your LinkedIn analytics dashboard daily so you can know which content is performing best and create more of the same. With a platform like LinkedIn, data-driven decisions will yield the most significant results and ensure that your marketing budget is going to the right campaigns.

• Get yourself a LinkedIn virtual assistant. Outsource some outreach help so you can search for and connect with the right individuals. Although this isn't direct advertising, it will still cost you money if you outsouIn essence, you would need to hire someone to go into your LinkedIn account and find the right and qualified connections from the companies you target. The targeting can be laser focused by the way, and you can narrow your 3rd-degree connections by locations, current company, etc. There's a lot of customization that can go into this search which will enable you to get in touch with the right people fast and it can all be done for free if you choose to put in the time yourself or you can outsource from platforms like Fiverr and Upwork. The idea here is to find individuals in an organization or professional field that you can build a relationship with.

Chapter 08: YouTube

Who is this platform great for?

Any type of business will do well on YouTube. This is the second most visited website in existence according to Alexa.

Regardless of your niche, this platform is bound to have access to your most ideal prospects. That's because it is by far the most popular and highly trafficked social platform. At the time of writing this, there are 1.9 billion logged-in users consuming content on this platform every month. That's literally half the Internet. And these people are watching a billion hours of video daily! I am certainly one of those daily Youtube consumers. Not a day goes by when I don't log in to learn a quick marketing tip or binge-watch documentaries about outer space. According to Cisco, they predict video will take up 82% of all Internet traffic by 2022. In a few years, it won't even matter what you're selling, if you don't have a strong video presence, your traffic will plummet.

YouTube is one of those platforms where you will find teenagers as well as retired folks spending time.

A few days ago while queuing at my local grocery store, I noticed the lady in front of me was killing time watching YouTube on her phone. She was watching this documentary called "Time Team." A seventy-something-year-old lady now chooses to spend her free time watching YouTube. And she was really into it, by the way, making remarks, laughing, etc. It was quite remarkable especially considering she was born in an era where cellphones didn't even exist let alone social media. All this to say, regardless of your products or services, YouTube is probably where you want to focus a lot more effort over the coming years.

Think back to the old lady at the grocery store. If you sell retirement products or services, how powerful would it be to have your ad pop up just before her favorite program comes on? This is the power available to you when you learn to use the channel for both paid and organic growth. Creating and posting video content on YouTube is a crucial way to boost visibility and gain credibility.

- The best types of content to post on YouTube

• Vlog

Vlogs or video blogs are exactly what the name suggests. These are the new antidotes to blog posts for those who've grown sick of them. They are easy and cheap to produce. What makes vlogs work so well is that they are personality driven and in a few seconds you can capture the attention of your audience in a way a blog post never could. Gary Vaynerchuck is a pro at vlogging and has one of the most popular vlogs in the marketing world. I recommend checking out his YouTube channel to get a test of how powerful this can be for you. You can simply document your journey as you grow and scale your business in this intimate and very engaging way.

• Interview content

I realize that many of the thought leaders we know have become that way through interviewing other thought leaders. Ever heard of Lewis Howes and his popular podcast "The School of Greatness" or the famous "social media marketing podcast"? Both these podcasts have grown in fame and made their founders successful by the mere act of interviewing other experts. What if you could start doing the same in your niche market?

Interviews seem to be the perfect way to inject some authority into your growing social media channels, and they also help build relationships with potential partners. These can help you produce lots of content, and if you do this well (and invite the right guests), you can leverage their knowledge to create more content for your brand.

• How to's and tutorials

And by this, I don't mean promotional tie ins and soft selling because your audience is smart enough to tell when they are being sold. I mean giving away valuable content without any hidden agenda. Start thinking of ways you can offer actionable resources to your target audience. For example, if you are a wellness brand, you could publish training videos that provide workout tips. If you're a nutrition brand, you could teach recipes and simple hacks for eating better.

• Product reviews

If you grow an audience that trusts you then doing product reviews can become a really popular content type, as they will find your reviews very useful. People have no time nowadays, so when you can give them great recommendations, they don't have to guess or figure things out on their own which makes them value your brand even more. Now I know what you're wondering. What types of reviews should you be doing? Well, the simple answer is this: Think of products, not in your line of work that is still very useful to your ideal customers. For example, if your ideal customers are parents, imagine how happy they would be if you recommended something that helps them with their parenting needs?

• Behind-the-scenes

We live in a digitally connected world, and people are more and more interested in working with businesses that seem more "human" and less "money making corporation." As such, the more you can put some personality into your business especially on YouTube, the better your growth rate will be. Video content that shares behind the scenes are one of the best ways to do this. Viewers can see your face, how you spend your day, your employees, how you interact with each other, how people in your company dress and the tone of voice the brand stands for. And the best part about this is that you don't need a professional team to create this for you. Informal videos are the best as they are more real and relatable to your audience. All you need to get started is your smartphone and the courage to hit record.

• Live streaming

People love instant gratification and that feeling of real-time connection with a brand. That's why Live streaming is doing so well across many of the social networks, and the same is true on YouTube. Use live streaming to broadcast a new product launch, do a live Q&A, teach people how to do something and so much more. You are only limited by your level of creativity.

- Tips For Organic Growth On YouTube

• Customize your channel to match your brand style and identity. As soon as a new visitor comes to your channel, they should immediately have a feel for your brand, and it needs to be congruent with your other social media networks and website. Use colors, images, links and other relevant information that helps visually express what your brand does.

• Design attractive thumbnails that are eye-catching and in harmony with your brand identity. When dealing with a blog, we all know the headline is the most important thing. With video, however, you need a great title as well as a thumbnail because that image makes up for 50% of your headline success. Choose a thumbnail that compliments your headline title and helps tell a story.

• Choose the best and most relevant keywords. Don't just go for what you think is right; focus on what your ideal audience is already searching for on the platform. You can use a tool like KewordTool.io for YouTube as well as Google keyword research. This shouldn't just be a one-timeendeavor; it must be done for every video you publish.

• Be intentional with your video titles. This is especially important if you care about SEO at all. People search on YouTube the same way they do on Google, using phrases and keywords. If you don't put some thought into the title and description you run the risk of not showing up when your ideal audience searches for the very solution you provide. And because Google owns YouTube, ranking high on these platforms gives you a boost on your overall Google ranking.

• Transcribe your video content. This is especially important for businesses because YouTube being a video platform doesn't leave much room for keyword-rich text. Savvy marketers are finding a way around this curve ball by offering a transcript at the bottom of the video.

• Experiment with YouTube cards. Strategically insert various types of C.T.As (call to action) in your video. This can be watching a follow-up video, watching the latest or most popular content, taking a poll, a lead magnet download or any other attractive offer. If you are going to experiment with this, however, it is important to do it tastefully. Don't overdo it. Try to use them either at the beginning or the end of your video and only have one call to action per video. Too many choices often lead to inaction.

• Collaborate with influencers and other relevant influencers so you can expand your reach. Viewers on YouTube really like seeing collaborative videos. Find popular channels that offer something complimentary to your business but still have the same audience you'd love to reach and try to pitch an idea for collaboration.

• Leverage Quora's traffic by answering their pressing questions on a video. Tapping into the power of Quora is a great way to generate more organic traffic and introduce people to your business. Questions are often used on YouTube as queries, so when you can find the most popular ones on Quora, you can easily get people to come to watch your video. And over time, you will rank higher for that question within YouTube. Find high volume - low competition Quora questions, provide immediate value on your YouTube video and link it as your answer on Quora.

• Promote your published video on other social media platforms. But don't just copy paste your video link on Facebook, Twitter and LinkedIn, customize the post to match the natural flair of each platform. Try different styles of formats for different social channels and tailor make it to suit the preferences of those who usually hang out on those platforms.

• Publish your content consistently and be patient with the process. This is probably the number one thing no ever emphasizes, and yet it's the reason behind most of the success stories you get to hear about YouTube. There are many clickbait articles on Internet today telling you how frequently you should publish and at what exact hour of the day but the truth is, the only way to grow and succeed with YouTube marketing is to become consistent. Decide on a specific strategy for YouTube, and a publishing frequency then stick to it for at least 12 months.

• Do outreach to increase your video exposure.
This is something common with blogs but can still apply with video content. When you publish a video, do a Google Search to find the relevant articles that also rank for the same keywords you used. Show the bloggers your video and suggest they embed it into their article. Not everyone will say yes, but some will and those are the right ones to help you expand your reach and even consider doing more collaborations with.

• Be more human and interactive. Instead of being a cold, serious and boring brand talking about why people should hire you or buy your product, create content that is inspiring, motivational, informative or entertaining. The more you focus on adding value first, the more receptive your audience will be to the content you create and your brand.

• Actively respond and engage in the YouTube community. As with all other social media channel, you must respond and interact with your community. This is more so the case in the YouTube community where engagement is everything. That goes beyond just the people who watch and comment on your videos. You need to have a list of channels that are on your watchlist. Frequently watch their videos, comment, like and support other video creators on YouTube. Connect with those that resonate with you most on other social media networks and nurture those relationships.

• Use data to determine whether you should be translating your most popular videos into other languages. YouTube has launched local versions in more than 88 countries, and you can easily navigate it in 76 different languages covering 95% of the Internet population. By going through your channel's demographic data, you can be able to tell if it's worth translating to a specific language (depending on how big an audience you have for that particular language). Using platforms like Fiverr and Upwork you can easily translate and transcribe into languages you can barely speak.

- Tips For Paid Advertising Success On YouTube

• Set up your ad campaign right. Don't just wing this! YouTube ads are way more sophisticated than Facebook or Instagram ads so take the necessary classes to educate yourself on how to run ads successfully on this platform. Adwords offer lots of useful information and training.

• Carefully craft you Call-to-action. Make sure it's simple, easy to spot and compelling.

• Use the skippable "in-stream ads" especially if you're just starting out. These get you the most visibility, and they quickly train you into knowing what grabs your audience attention and what doesn't. The great news is that if people do skip over the ad, you don't pay anything if the video is under 30 seconds. This type of ad will force the viewer to pay attention to you and interrupt what they were thinking about. If they take action, then it's a sure sign your ad is on the right track. I recommend pairing this ad with a value-adding landing page to get people into your funnel.

• Test to make sure your funnel converts well. This ties in very well with the tip previously shared. There's nothing worse than getting people to click over and then losing them once they land on your website. Keep your landing page copy and messaging congruent, simple, actionable and focused on delivering on your promise.

• Experiment with different styles and formats for your video ads. Try explainer videos, how to videos, interviews, talking head, etc. You can even test a TV commercial style YouTube video. Get creative with this and have fun!

• Get clear on your campaign objectives and then test a few of the different options that YouTube offers. For example, if you're looking to raise brand awareness, then a TrueView in-stream or discovery ad might help you get better results. If however, you want high quality leads then consider sponsored cards as well. There's really no right way of doing this. Just choose a few ad formats, run them for a short period of time, compare performance and double down on the ones that perform the best.

• Create different campaigns if you are working with both In-stream and discovery ad formats. This is because they are fundamentally performing different functions. In-stream ads play before, during or after other videos. Discovery ads appear next to related YouTube videos as part of YouTube search results or alongside other content across the Display Network. As such, you need a different budget and strategy as well as a separate campaign so you can easily monitor both.

• Across every social media network, I have mentioned, retargeting or "remarketing" as it's often known in YouTube marketing remains the most effective way to grow your audience and increase sales. Mainly because you are remarketing to an audience, you're certain cares about what you have to say. These people have already expressed their interest in your business by clicking on your link.

• Make your ads less salesy and more natural. If your ad comes across too salesy, it most likely won't do well on any social platform. YouTube is no exception. The more natural, human and personal the content feels, the more likely people will engage with it. Which leads me to my next tip.

• Use storytelling on your video ads. Figure out a way to incorporate a lot of storytelling into your video content. Match your personality and your brand identity with the type of storytelling you tell. For example, if you love humor, use it to your advantage and create compelling storytelling ads that make your audience laugh.

• Invest in understanding your ideal audience. The mere fact that billions of people from all walks of life are actively engaged in this platform daily means you could easily try to reach everyone. That would be a mistake. Marketing to everyone means you're connecting with no one. Be very targeted with your audience and speak their language in your content. Evoke emotions and keep that small pocket of people captivated and wanting more. This is how you will end up growing a highly profitable audience and business.

Chapter 09: Twitter

Which type of business should be actively engaged on this platform?

Twitter is a great place to grow your business, especially if you are in travel, hospitality, media, sales, and marketing, entertainment or any other type of niche that regularly deals with events. But you should know, things move really fast on Twitter. The average lifespan of a tweet is said to be around 18 minutes (4 x shorter lifespan than anything you could post on Facebook). So when it comes to Twitter, making things stick or trying to pass on long-winded messages will not serve you. Making an impact on this channel is about being short, sweet and punch. Designed initially as a micro blogging tool inspired by the short message services (SMS), Twitter works best when you can leverage it as a way to keep people in the loop about your brand, share entertaining and fun tweets, handle customer service needs and network with the right industry influencers.

I am assuming you already have the right Twitter handle and you've worked some magic on your profile, the next thing to do is to start tweeting when it's most appropriate for your audience so you can get maximum reach. Before I share tips that will help you with both organic and paid ads success, here are a few more things that make this platform worth investing in.

The magic that Twitter brings is the fact that you have the power of "stalking" your potential clients on this platform without the uncomfortable tension that usually accompanies in-person networking events. When I say stalking I mean this in the nicest way and I trust your boundaries and ethics are well in place here.

Twitter is a great online networking spot for businesses because it's where your competition and your customers are probably sharing quick conversations. These conversations can be tremendously valuable to you and your business because you can see what your competition is focused on as well as customer feedback in real time. Two key tactics are pretty useful especially on Twitter if you want to find information and possible clients. You can search by category or by Keyword, hashtag, phrase, and Tag. Using these tactics, you can find companies that are relevant to you and individuals that you want to connect with. Of course, there are also Twitter tools that can assist you in identifying influential industry power hitters so make sure you familiarize yourself with some of the tools your business could be using.

- The best types of content to post on Twitter

If you want to do well on Twitter and drive lots of high-value traffic to your funnel, stop spending so much time tweeting about yourself. I recommend making only one out of every five tweets about your business or brand. So if you post ten times a day, then only 2 tweets should directly be about your business. I have a simple formula to help me stay on track with my tweeter posting.

Website Link Tweet - this type of tweet has a call to action that links back to a website, blog article, press release, lead magnet or something that I know is valuable to my audience. It offers an opportunity for my followers to interact more with my business and brand.

Industry News - This type of tweet helps establish you as an expert in your niche and shows that you're in the know. It has nothing to do with your personal or business brand. The main intention is to share something very relevant to your audience about your industry so they can learn what's new.

Quick Question - This tweet is fast, generates engagement and invites real conversation. When creating these types of tweets for my clients, or me I like to mix things up. Sometimes the question asked is brand related (depending on the niche I am trying to reach) and sometimes it's just for human connection. Something as simple as asking "what do you prefer, tea or coffee?"

Networking Tweets - The name says it all. This is mostly when you want to start a rapport and make a connection with someone you value. It can be an influencer, celebrity or a potential prospect. Be thoughtful about the tweets you create for networking purposes and make sure they are specific, meaningful and adding value to the receiver, whether they retweet and respond or not.

Here are a few content types to experiment with:

• Trending topics.

Once you understand your target market and what they find interesting, get in the habit of sharing trendy but relevant content so that you can create a conversation around something people are already talking about on the platform. As a brand, it's your job to find that sweet spot between what's trending and what's relevant to your audience as well as your mission.

• Infographics

Publish useful and aesthetically pleasing infographics around your topic of expertise. By using infographics in your tweets, you share valuable information in an exciting way that would otherwise not happen with the limited characters offered by the platform.

• Gifs

These are fun, quirky and also super effective on Twitter. They are really great at grabbing attention especially on Twitter where things happen really fast. I find them to be a cost-effective alternative to videos, especially when promoting new materials and it helps you play around with your own creativity.

• Videos

We all know that video is performing well on almost every major platform, so it's no wonder the same is true on Twitter. On this platform, your video content actually plays automatically making it a highly effective way to grab attention especially when it comes to attracting new potential customers. You can use videos to share quick tips, teach "how to" content, make announcements, share promotion and so on.

• Twitter polls

Many brands are using Twitter polls as a marketing tool for product research and promotion. It's also a great way to know what your already existing customers really want to hear from you or improvements they would like to see on your products or services.

- Tips For Organic Growth On Twitter

• Find the sweet spot for your business.

Every business will have to customize its own Twitter identity because no two companies are identical. As a general rule, you want to find the overlap between what your target audience wants to hear and things that promote your business. I have seen talking about the benefits your customers will experience as a result of your products or service to be great Tweeting material. Give useful information, answer questions, use stories and case studies as this will help demonstrate value to your customers and even win over new ones.

• Create Tweets around a link that drives people to your blog, landing page or website. Make sure the headline is attractive enough so that people will want to click on it.

• Increase your frequency of tweeting image-based content. People love looking at pictures (even on Twitter). Include images in your tweets whenever possible.

• Use more video content to increase reach and engagement on your Twitter. You can add videos to your Twitter timeline but not directly. So I recommend uploading them on YouTube or Facebook first and then linking back to them on your tweet. Of course, always remember to include some context that will make people want to click.

• Use Vine to shoot 6-second videos. This is a new feature from Twitter that allows you to take those short videos and play them on an endless loop inside Twitter. This can be a great way to tell your brand story, as the videos created here will be added to your photo gallery on Twitter.

• Use Hashtags to expand your audience and connect with new prospects and influencer. When you spot a tweet with a relevant hashtag, click on it to see a list of all tweets that include the same hashtag so you can start connecting with people who don't yet know your brand. Check out their accounts and as you find people you'd like to connect with, engage with them. Follow them or create a Twitter list for them so you can continue to nurture the relationship.

• Use Twitter Advanced Search to find people near your location. You can use the "Places" feature to identify your location by city or zip code. Twitter will display a list of people who are tweeting near that location, and you can then leverage this information and create a list of targeted potential customers that you want to start engaging with.

• Build a Twitter community. Using the right tools, you can analyze who is following you and reach out to those targeted individuals, inviting them into your closed community where you can continue to serve them and nurture that relationship. This can, in turn, make your Twitter marketing very effective.

• Post several times a day. Neil Patel shared an experiment that he and his team conducted on Twitter. They posted once a day for seven days at the end of which they had 749 visitors only.

Then they posted 40 times a day for another week at the end of which they had 5623 visitors. Clearly, his results show that posting more frequently on Twitter will get you more traffic from Twitter. Now, I know, 40 times is just crazy especially if you don't have a team helping out. Start with at least 10 times a day, monitor the progress and adjust accordingly.

• Measure and track your Twitter performance over time. As with all social networks, without data and analysis, it will be hard knowing what's working and what doesn't. It's easier to grow your audience and get better results when you have solid data backing up your Twitter strategies.

- Tips For Paid Advertising Success On Twitter

• Do your research and check what your competitors are doing and what's working for them.
• Gather social proof. If more people are interacting with your ad, more people will start following you. Aim for at least a few hundred likes and shares. You can choose to first target an audience that isn't too competitive and costs less to reach them and then you can go all in with a bigger budget to a more competitive target audience.
• Make sure the only clickable element in your ad is the call to action that you want people to take. Which means you should not include any Twitter mentions or hashtags on your ads.
• Target mobile users since most people on Twitter access the platform through their smartphones. You'll need to ensure that the option is ticked before publishing the advertisement.
• Keep refreshing your content every few days. Update your ad creative and copy so you can keep your audience engaged and avoid ad fatigue.

• Remove keywords, follower groups, and tweets that are not performing well and turn off the campaigns that in general start underperforming.
• Continue to experiment with different variations. Do split tests (if you know how to do this right), so you can optimize your ad and drive more traffic to your funnel. Remember, as you do your split tests to change only one thing at a time.

• Keep monitoring the campaigns that are doing well, modify your bids and increase ad spend on the ones that merit a higher budget. This, of course, implies you are doing your tracking and measuring exceptionally well. The more you know how to read the data and take immediate action, the better results you can expect from your Twitter campaigns.

Chapter 10: Pinterest And Google+

Pinterest

Pinterest is a fantastic site especially if you're an e-commerce business selling products. The first thing you need to know is that you need to have a business account on Pinterest to use this platform's full potential. You also get different terms of services, educational marketing materials, analytics, rich pins and so much more. This makes it possible for you to measure and monitor and maximize your efforts on this often overlooked platform. On average, each pin on Pinterest is worth around seventy-eight cents in sales, drives two site visits and six-page views and is repinned around ten times.

But of course, to experience such numbers, you need to build some momentum and post several times a day if you want to enjoy the high engagement promised by the platform.

Google+

It might seem as though Facebook, Instagram, and Twitter are all you need and that Google+ is a waste of time, but if you are at all interested in improving your SEO then you should give some attention to this platform as well.

This isn't just about setting up an account on Google+. In fact, if that's all you do, then you're right; it's probably just a waste of time. Google+ has a lot to offer, and if you are a serious business looking for longevity, then you need to go beyond posting updates once in a while. Google+ can be a valuable platform for any small business. And if you are in hospitality, travel, entertainment, sports or if you are a local business then you definitely need to have an active business page.

Google+ requires a different mindset if you want it to work for you. Start to view it as a place to have a conversation and gather feedback about your products or services. It's not an advertising platform (something many small business owners keep forgetting); so constant self-promotion will lead nowhere.

- The best types of content to post on Pinterest and Google+On Pinterest...

•How-to and DIY content do great on this platform. People on Pinterest are by default overly ambitious and love to create things on their own, organize, paint, build, etc. Or at least that's the story being told by their Pinterest boards. As such, visual tutorials and DIY projects and crafts as the King of the Hill in the land known as Pinterest.

• Food and drinks/recipes are among the top performers on Pinterest. This is also one of the most popular categories, so it's no wonder visually appealing recipes will get lots of attention. Whatever your style is (healthy, junk and everything in between) if adequately executed will find an audience here. People love recipes no matter how ridiculous. Just make sure you invest in high-quality pictures to really showcase your goodies.

• Cute images. In Pinterest land, there is no such thing as too much cuteness. Animal pics (yes those ones that make you feel all warm and fuzzy inside) are at the top of the list. Do you have a cute puppy? A cat that makes you laugh? Would a baby fit in your product? Can a kitten enjoy what you sell? These adorable little creatures can be your golden ticket to massive sales!

• Humorous posts as long as you do it right will work well on Pinterest. And it's not so much about making your product funny. Instead, it's about leveraging your witty, funny personality. Get creative here.

• Scenic images with or without motivational quotes. People love them. They love to see pictures of places they wish to visit or a beautiful motivational quote with a relaxing background of somewhere exotic. Now, this type of content may not naturally align with your brand or product so take some time to brainstorm concepts that align with your brand "as a lifestyle choice."

That should get you on the right path with content for the next few weeks. Let's switch gears and see the types of content you can create for your Google+.

On Google+...

• If you want to get some attention on Google+, try using Gifs and cinemagraphs. On this platform, they can easily be uploaded shared and viewed just like a regular image. But I do recommend using these as part of more substantial content and not as a standalone with no context.

• YouTube videos are a must on this platform. First of all, you can embed YouTube videos inside Google+ posts. Also, YouTube comments are integrated with Google+, which means a viewer has the default option to have that comment shared into their Google+ stream. This increases the likelihood of your video going viral.

• Use rich link share to post Industry related news. This will automatically attach a featured post to the top of a headline link. One of the benefits of sharing valuable content this way even if you didn't publish the original piece is the platform's "Do-Follow" status. This means that any PageRank or "Google juice" the Google+ post URL accumulates will be passed along to the page in which the post is linked.

• Create images with Google+ stories. Did you even know this platform has this feature? Very few people do, and they are an incredible opportunity for your brand to stand out from the crowd. A great way to use Google+ stories is to take lots of pictures on your next conference so that you can create a Google+ story from there. Then share the Google+ story with an article to recap the event. If you can notify or even tag other influencers who attended the event. This will help give your content way more exposure.

- Tips For Organic Growth and paid ads On Pinterest and Google+

• Add save buttons to your site so people can Pin your content with just a click, even if they don't have the Pinterest browser button installed.

• If you want to do well on Pinterest, you must learn to create popular pins. This is only possible if you understand what your followers are searching for while on the platform. Find your most relevant and most popular categories and create boards around them. There are various categories (from DIY crafts to Tattoos and everything in between) so pick your categories, create beautiful imagery, use the right dimensions recommended by the platform and make sure it is a high-resolution picture.

• Focus on creating attractive visuals, as this is a highly visual medium. Think about creative ways to showcase your product and your brand visually. Pinterest studied the performance of over 50,000 promoted Pins and discovered that lifestyle images generally outperform product images. For example, fashion and style Pins showcasing products being used in real life saw thirty percent more clickthroughs and one hundred and seventy percent higher checkout rates than those showcasing the product alone. According to Pinterest, pins that show someone using your product or service are 67% more likely to drive offline sales.

• Add context to your visuals through excellent copy. It is true that Pinterest is mostly a visual platform, but if you want to drive real engagement, those images need to have thoughtful words specially crafted to get your viewers to click through to the content on your site. Use the description section to add context and meaning to your visuals. Quality copywriting will get Pinners excited about following and interacting with your brand within and outside of Pinterest.

• Make your texts keyword rich but don't overdo it. Applying a little keyword research and incorporating the keywords you want to rank for can help your Pins appear in search, but please make sure you use them appropriately.

• Pin consistently. And even though Pinterest recommends that you Pin something at least once per day during evenings and weekends for U.S based brands, I encourage you to do it multiple times a day. Buffer released an article sharing their best practices on Pinterest and revealed that sharing five times a day (at least) worked really well for them.
The more you Pin, the greater your reach and visibility to a new audience.

• Use Rich Pins but don't overdo it. These are posts that have extra information on the Pin itself. Rich Pins are great because they pull metadata from your site to provide additional details about what Pinners will find when they click on a Pin. They are available for recipes, apps, articles, place, and products. For example, a Rich Pin for articles will include the headline, name of the author, the date the article was published and story description.

They also specifically indicate that the link points to an article and include a call to action button that says, "Read it." This can be a great way to get the right people who are interested in what you have to offer to visit your website or blog but as I said, use this feature appropriately.

• Experiment with buyable Pins. This is even more effective if you run an e-commerce store because it enables users to purchase your product directly off a pin. These Pins work on mobile and web browsers, and they appear in the same places as a Promoted Pin would. The only difference is items in the image are tagged with white dots that can be tapped or clicked on to display and link to product information.
As pinners browse the platform and create wish lists, they can see your product details, price, and description. If they like it, they can purchase it all with a few quick clicks on their mobile device.
Pinterest recommends that images should be tagged with four to six dots. Each dot should be linked directly to the product's page, but if that's not possible, then Pinterest suggests finding one exact match and other close matches. There's a tagging tool offered by the platform to help you create Buyable Pins. If increased sales if what you're after, then this is a must for your business.

• Boost your best content with Pinterest promoted pins. These are a great way to get your Pins in front of a new audience and to give your brand long term exposure because you can keep getting organic clicks long after your promo ad runs its course. It's also a quick way to drive traffic directly to your landing page because when a user clicks on the link of a promoted pin, he or she is taken straight to a landing page.

• Test out promoted carousels especially if you sell products. These feature two to five images that Pinners can swipe through. Each card in a promoted carousel ad can feature a different picture, title, description and landing page.
• Create a video campaign on Pinterest. These are great for brand awareness campaign and a perfect way to tell your brand's story or your product launch story. Promoted video pins are just like promoted pins except the static image is replaced with video, and they too appear in

the home feed, search results and the "more like this" section under a Pin close-up. One thing I do recommend here is that you create a video that's not dependent on audio because most viewers watch the video without sound on this platform. There are two types of video you can create here: Max width and standard. Standard width video is the same size as a regular Pin. Max width video spreads across the feed minimizing distraction from competing Pins, which can be great for getting the attention of your new audience. But be aware the max width will cost more.

• If you have an app, experiment with promoted app pins. Promoted App Pins allows Pinners to download your mobile app directly from Pinterest. These are mobile-only ads and could work really well for your brand since 80% of Pinterest traffic comes from mobile devices. These ads look just like any other Pinterest ad with the only difference being that the link can only lead back to a valid iTunes or Google Play app store URL.

• Analyze your results regularly and optimize on the tactics and posts that do well. Develop a data-driven approach to Pinterest for your business even though it's a smaller social networking platform. This will help you optimize your presence and predict your success better. More right clicks and impressions lead to more traffic and sales! And don't worry too much about getting third-party tools. Use the built-in Pinterest Analytics for business, and it will show you how every post is performing.

• With Google+ you want to make sure you add recommended links. In the "About" tab you have the option to add links to your blog and business homepage. I also suggest adding a link to some of the offers you want to promote.

• Add photos on your Google+ to showcase company events, employee photos, behind the scenes pictures, product photos, community events and any other informative or entertaining image you can think of.

• Use Google+ to provide valuable industry insights. Answer any questions users might have about your brand and take time to engage with the community regularly. Being active on this platform can actually help you rank at the top of Google search results. What's even better is that even your status updates can appear in search results especially if you carefully sprinkle some rich keywords into your updates.

• Occasionally offer limited-time discounts and monitor the response you get from this. Don't use this tactic too often; otherwise, it will stop working for you.

• Use Google hangouts if it aligns with your brand style and if you have a big enough presence on the platform. Depending on your niche you could use this for Q&A or exclusive interviews with influencers and industry leaders. These videos will then get posted to YouTube allowing even more people to watch it and creating valuable content for your YouTube community.

• Find creative ways to engage with and connect with influencers. This may not be a huge social network, but many brands and influencers actively hang out on this platform. See if you can find those relevant to your niche or industry and find thoughtful ways of engaging with them. Perhaps you can create some value adding content that attracts their interest and causes them to share your content and expose your brand to their wider audience. There's no telling what can happen if you put in some effort and create a presence on this platform. It may not be as appealing as Facebook and Instagram, but given the fact that Google owns it, I'd say it's worth having your brand well represented there as well.

Chapter 11: Tips For Content Creation

This book would, of course, be very incomplete if we didn't dedicate a chapter on content creation and how to organize yourself best so that you can always produce fresh, high-quality stuff. Content marketing has become one of the most powerful digital marketing strategies regardless of your niche, and when combined with social media, results can be incredible.

In today's world where so much content is being produced daily, it's not enough to quickly create and push out content to your audience. unless, of course, you don't really care about creating meaningful connections with your audiSince this book is primarily intended to help you leverage social media marketing to grow and increase revenue, creating content must become very intentional and purposeful. You can't just settle for okay or even good content. You need amazing content that helps your ideal potential customer take notice of your brand. A minimalist approach to your content creation (meaning that you just do the bare minimum) will get you nowhere so let me share a few pointers on how you can make your social media content gain maximum exposure.

• First, you must understand the psychology behind the sharing of content on social media.

If you don't know why your audience shares things on social media, you won't be able to create content that resonates and draws people into your business. A report from The New York Times Customer Insight Group found that people are sharing content on social media for five main reasons.

#1. 84% of the people are sharing because it is a way for them to support a cause or issue they care about.

Try this: Create content that helps them believe in something worthwhile. Give them a common shared goal, show them how much you value and respect them and let them feel like it's more than just making a sale when it comes to your brand.

#2. 78% of people are sharing information online because it lets them stay connected to people they would otherwise not stay in touch with. It gives them something to connect over.

Try this: Leverage your brand and social platforms and become a reliable resource for your audience so they can use your information or community to connect with people they want to keep connecting with. When people feel safe around you, they will want to bring on others that they care about as well.

#3. 69% of people are sharing information because it allows them to feel more involved in the world.

Try this: Be more engaged and interactive with your audience. There's nothing worse than seeing comments on an Instagram post or YouTube channel and no response from the business. If someone leaves you a comment, sends a message or responds to a tweet, let them know that you value them and that he or she is important in your eyes.

#4. 68% of people are sharing to give other people in their circle of influence a better sense of who they are and what they care about.

Try this: Create content that helps your audience define themselves. You have different customer types, so I encourage you to create content that helps them self-identify.

#5. 49% of people say sharing allows them to inform others of products they care about and potentially change their opinions or encourage a specific action.

Try this: Create a balanced mix of content on your social platforms where you talk about your own brand, offer useful and valuable information and also share great content from reputable sources. Let people see you as a trusted authority and someone who cares about delivering the best content whether or not it ties directly into a sale for your business. This is how you establish longevity in your business and increase referrals for your products or services.

As you can imagine, there are lots of lessons we can all learn from this information. It means the better we understand why our audience reacts a certain way to our content, and what drives their behavior as they socialize with us online, the more empowered we are to create content that does really well. This isn't meant to be guesswork. The more you observe, listen to and interact with your growing audience, the more power you have to create content that converts them into paid customers because you'll be producing what you know works. Do you know why your audience shares content online?

That's a great place to start when it comes to mapping out and organizing the content types you'll be producing over the coming months.

Now, before we share tips on how to organize yourself for production, let's discuss the three major content creation types that you must produce consistently regardless of the platforms you choose to invest in.

- Written Content

• Blog - Truly one of the most popular ways to create written content and for a good reason. If your business doesn't yet have a blog, I strongly recommend starting one immediately. Not only does it help with the customer journey and adding value to your audience on social media, but it also helps with your long-term SEO efforts. Companies that blog are said to have 97% more inbound links and B2B marketers say they generate 67% more leads through their blogs.

• eBooks - writing an eBook is a great way to share industry insights, showcase your expertise and add value to your customer even before they choose to work with you. This doesn't have to be a long formal eBook, get creative, and think more about what your buying customer would be interested in learning from you. You can even outsource it if you don't feel confident to write it on your own.

• Email marketing

Emails are still a very effective way to reach your ideal customer consistently. It can be as simple or complex as your marketing team can handle. You can send a regular broadcast of curated and original content to your email list or opt for something like an ongoing soap opera sequence.

• Case studies

Case studies and testimonials are a highly effective way to influence purchases. Like customer success stories, case studies prove that what you offer actually works. It's a great way of convincing your customer to try your product or service and if you know where to place them on your website they can also help with SEO.

• FAQs

This is a great way to answer customer objections, concerns and can go a long way in advancing potential sales.

• Customer success stories

These are quickly becoming super valuable in building that know, like and trust factor with a new prospect. It's also a great way to brag about your business without actually doing it yourself. This can be as short as a one-page document or several pages in length. Share your customer stories and illustrate how your business has helped a specific customer become successful. You can also use this to highlight special applications or uses for your products and services.

• Infographics

These types of content are fun, colorful and a great way for you to educate your audience and provide useful information. It's even more appealing for businesses that need to describe what they do visually or for brands that deal with data (like statistics) so that people can have a better understanding of why something is valuable of how something works.

• White papers

These are similar to eBooks with the main and probably the only difference being that they tend to be more information dense and data-driven. Most business owners who will benefit from this type of content will be in the B2B space.

• Checklists/ Recipes

Checklists, worksheets, cheat sheets, templates, recipes, and so many others are created to offer quick benefits to your customer. Depending on your niche and the audience you serve, you may choose to create some or all of these content assets. They are quick and easy to create and promote, yet still, provide significant value for your target audience.

- Video Content

• Vlogging

This is just like regular blogging except instead of writing, you speak directly to the camera.

• Tutorials

These types of content are loved by people regardless of the industry because people love learning how to do or be something.

• Live streaming

You can use your smartphone or computer to start a live broadcast, even record your own reality show and get your audience to journey with you as you build and scale your business. This is a fun, interactive, real and raw way of connecting with your audience.

•Interviews

One of the easiest ways to position your brand and yourself as an authority on social media is to be seen with other experts. Use video to record your conversations, interviews, and training with other experts in your space and you'll never run out of high-quality content to share.

• Webinar

This is another excellent way of leveraging the power of video. You can host a live webinar training people on your topic or showcasing your product. Just make sure the webinar is actually actionable and valuable for the attendees.

• Product demos.

Although few businesses think of this, I find it very useful because it shows your product in action while also making potential customers feel like they are getting an exclusive inside look. Make sure your product demonstration answers common questions and highlights key features so that shoppers can see how they get value from doing business with you.

- Audio Content

• Recorded audio blog posts

By taking your written content and turning it into recorded voice content, you can repurpose it and distribute it into other media platforms such as sound cloud. It's a smart way of ensuring your content goes a long way in reaching a broader audience.

• Solo Podcasting

Podcasting has become such a big trend, and more and more brands (even big brands) are setting up podcasting channels to engage with their audience. For many people commuting to work, this method of consuming content is efficient which means, your business might stand to benefit a lot if you start a podcast. Keep in mind though that similar to SEO, this requires long-term thinking.

• Interview podcast

With this type of audio content, you typically host a guest in a Q&A format where you get to ask them questions. You can create new questions for each guest you bring on or do a more traditional interview-style podcast where you always ask the same question. Podcasts like Entrepreneur On Fire have grown into profitable businesses leveraging this strategy.

These are just a few ways of leveraging content marketing. Make your own list of content types that resonate with you and start experimenting immediately. Now, I know you're wondering how to make sure all these ideas get implemented. To help you with that, let me share some quick hacks and tools that will streamline your content creation and distribution.

- How to effectively organize your social media marketing calendar

Whether you're a one-man show or working with a marketing team, it's essential to get into the habit of organizing your content and scheduling your calendar in advance.

The more you grow and scale your business, the more I recommend getting a robust marketing management solution like a Coschedule or other social media apps and scheduling tools but for now, all you need is a spreadsheet or a printed calendar, and you can be able to organize your social media calendar effectively.

Every business owner must have a way of planning which content will be shared, where it will be shared, a simple way of managing all campaigns and tracking deadlines. Staying organized with a calendar makes it much easier to save time and maintain consistency. And trust me, when you're working with limited resources, this is all the more crucial to have. To set up your first social media-marketing calendar, here are a few tips.

• Get a broad and general calendar. This calendar helps you focus on topics that actually matter to your audience. I suggest planning out this broad topic calendar four to six months out.

• Get a content calendar created. This is where you start diving into more detail and look at your topics so you can plan the exact content types (mentioned earlier in this chapter) that you know will resonate most with your audience. This can be blog posts, vlogs, eBooks, webinars, events or anything else you want to create and promote on social media. With this detailed plan, it is essential you assign a specific date where each piece should be published. If you can plan this out two to three months out, that will already give you a great head start and set you way ahead of other business owners.

• The next tip is to create your promotion calendar. This is the when and where of your social media marketing plan, and it's also where you start scheduling your messages, planning your emails and the other content that you'll be sharing. This part of your document needs to have the social media post copy, the related Image link and URL if it will include one. You can then assign a specific date for publication and of course, once published you can follow it up with the Google drive folder (the tip mentioned earlier in this book) that tracks and organizes all your "published" content in the various platforms you will advertise in.

• Now it's time to complete building your social media content strategy. Throughout this book, I have walked you through all the different things you must consider before deciding where you will invest your time and the kind of monitoring and measuring you will do. I even gave you simple exercises, questions to reflect on and templates to copy so that you don't walk away from our time together empty-handed. By now, if you've done the work, you're ready to start executing on all these ideas.

When it comes to your social media content strategy, keep things super simple. All you need to do now is figure out the content that works best for your chosen social network. Map out which content will be shared and where. Can you share the same piece of content on multiple channels? Yes, of course. But you must make sure your social media messages follow the best practices I shared.

Let's do a quick recap for the different social networks you can choose from:

• Facebook is more about sharing entertaining content. This is truly an entertainment hub where anything and everything goes. Since it's mostly about connecting with friends and family, you need to create content with that in mind. Post things that will engage your audience. Experiment with visual content, live video, recorded video, and images with messages that are less than 100 characters as well as long-form posts. Create fun quizzes, contests, and challenges. You can use links, share curated content and even cross promote.

• Instagram is at the time of writing this the platform where most engagement and it happens really fast. Aesthetics is everything when it comes to Instagram. Beautiful, sexy and transformational works really well here. Experiment with quote images, high-resolution photos, short videos, and Instagram stories.

• YouTube is the second most trafficked site on the Internet. Regardless of your business, you should definitely consider having an active YouTube channel. Experiment with vlogging, how-to and tutorials, product reviews if relevant, live streaming, interviews, etc. Focus on building a community around your channel and be responsive.

• LinkedIn is more professional. No cat videos, please! Share business-related content. Experiment with industry news, thought leadership content, productivity hacks, and career advancement tips. Share posts with short messages, images with statistics, meaningful quotes, videos, etc. Make sure every post is carefully thought out and give people a reason to engage with your content. I also encourage you to publish articles on the LinkedIn publishing platform. Even though this is a more serious platform where the main interest is business, I don't want you to focus solely on promoting your business. Build real relationships and strive to be the brand that's known for being customer focused.

• Twitter is a microblogging site where everything happens really fast. It's a great way to show a little personality while still remaining professionally focused. News travels fast, and you need to make sure your posts are quick and attractive. Share useful business tips that will draw your readers in. Use visuals like Gifs, Images, and quotes. Experiment with video, Twitter polls, and links as well. When you do use links be tasteful about it and balance it out with content that adds lots of value to your audience. This is also a great platform for sharing curated content and retweeting. Make sure you adhere to their character limitation and implement the tips I shared earlier when balancing out the content mix in your strategy.

• Google+ will work well for you if you combine a bit of personality with lots of professional content. It is great for sharing technical how-to content and company stories. Think of it as a great platform where your customers can get their questions answered, learn more about the technical side of your offer and also get a behind-the-scenes experience. Experiment with Gifs, videos, blog posts, photos, and Google+ stories. You can also try long-form content here. I see them performing really well, probably because of the network's natural SEO juice.

• Pinterest is a visual platform where you get to create attractive visuals for your product or service to tell a story and invite people to buy directly. This is where cute sells, so don't be shy to experiment with all your unicorn ideas. Brainstorm creative ways that you can draw in a larger audience with Pins and boards that promote your brand. You can also curate content that adds value to your audience. Think infographics, comics, custom photography, memes and other types of aesthetically pleasing images.

Chapter 12: Next Steps

If you want to dominate social media in 2019, grow your audience faster than ever before and translate that into annual revenue, it's now within your reach. With the insights, growth hacks, tips and easy to copy templates that have been shared throughout this book, there are no more excuses. It's time to execute and reach for your goals.

We have gone through all the major platforms, the best practices for both organic and paid advertising to grow your audience as well as the top performing content that you should be experimenting with. The more strategic and organized you get with your social media marketing the easier it will be to optimize growth and engagement regardless of your specific niche.

- Setting realistic goals for social media

If you want to scale your business and optimize your social media marketing, then you must set clear goals to help guide your strategy. Every platform you choose to invest in must have clearly identified goals, a marketing strategy and key performance indicators that you or your marketing team monitor.

First, conduct a social media audit.

Second, set clear and S.M.A.R.T goals. Make sure your social media goals align with your overall business goals and strive to make your goals achievable and realistic. For example, if you currently have 5000 visitors coming to your website each month, setting a goal of 1,000000 visitors a month in the next 30 days is obviously doing yourself and your marketing team a disservice. Shoot for something that stretches you and can be attained within that time.

Third, decide the KPI's that are important to you depending on your overall business goal.

Fourth, choose a goal-setting framework and create content and social media strategy. Stick to your chosen plan and structure until you see results.

Last but not least, gain customer and market insights as you continue to collect and monitor the data and feedback coming in.

Social media works if you know how to work it. And the biggest secret is that there is no secret! The human you are, and the more you show people you genuinely care about them, the more responsive people will be.

You need to make the first move and show people on social media that your brand isn't just interested in making a quick buck. Business is about making a profit, and social media is about socializing. Find a way to blend the two, and you will thrive in this digitally connected economy.

5 Startling Social Media Marketing trends that will Dominate 2019

As we come to the end of this book and the beginning of your social media marketing adventure, it's only right to end with a few smart insights that you should be considering throughout the year.

Insight #1: Use storytelling and share moments that matter with your audience. Stories are the way to go if you want to win in marketing this year so leverage them as much as possible.

Insight #2: Focus on engagement, building community and socializing. Don't use social media as a broadcasting medium. People are savvy, and they know when they are just being used. Offer authentic communication that helps people connect and build meaningful relationships.

Insight #3: Show your audience you care about them. If you don't show your tribe that you love and care about them, your social media marketing efforts will not result in higher sales. Be as responsive as you can to the people currently following you. If you can shift your focus from broadcasting to building one to one relationships, you'll get a much bigger ROI with your social media strategy.

Insight #4: Consider bringing in micro-influencers and other more prominent influencers to help push your brand out into the online world. Connecting with non-competitive influencers, business owners, thought leaders and other relevant micro influencers could open up many opportunities for you.

Insight #5: In-the-moment content will become a significant trend this year. This means that you need to experiment with content that connects your audience with the human side of your business. Experimentation is what will help you know the best direction to take. For example, if you're a coffee shop, you can start shooting short videos demonstrating how your coffee is brewed fresh. If you're a service business, you might give people short raw footage of the team hard at work. Whatever you choose to do, make sure it's real, authentic and meaningful to your brand and the audience consuming it.

And there you have it, now it's time to put the book down, roll up your sleeves and start implementing your social media marketing strategy.

Additional Resources:

Here are some useful links if you want to dive even deeper into this topic.

How to create a social media marketing strategy for 2019 and beyond:
https://buffer.com/library/social-media-marketing-strategy

18 reasons why your business needs a social media marketing: https://www.contentfac.com/9-reasons-social-media-marketing-should-top-your-to-do-list/

Exactly how small businesses can use Social Media for growth!-https://blog.hootsuite.com/social-media-tips-for-small-business-owners/

Effective Facebook AD strategies for 2019- https://www.garyvaynerchuk.com/effective-facebook-advertising-strategies-for-2019/

Personal Branding Strategies

The Ultimate Practical Guide to Branding And Marketing Yourself Online Through Instagram, YouTube, Facebook and Twitter And How To Utilize Advertising on Social Media

By Gary Clyne

Table of Contents

Section One

"Social media changes the relationship between companies and customers from master and servant, to peer-to-peer."

-Jay Baer

Introduction:

There is a rising new class of online influencers who are turning social media into a lucrative platform for selling brands. Would you like to make lots of cash, enjoy a glamorous lifestyle and travel the world as well? Then you've come to the right place!

Scroll through some of these highly paid social media influencers, and you'll see how glamorous their lives seem to be. Posting stunning photos and showing off some of the best locations in the world to their thousands or at times millions of followers. It's no wonder many people want to become online influencers.

If you've spent some time on YouTube, Instagram or Facebook I'm sure you've seen how some individuals appear to be living a dreamy vacation lifestyle. Taking pictures in exotic beaches like Bora Bora, Bali and Maldives, posing like fashionistas in front of the Arch de Triomphe in Paris or enjoying winter in a beautiful cabin somewhere on the French Alps.

Most social media influencers tend to include on their captions information about their outfits, accessories, and the prestigious locations they are visiting along with a long list of hashtags. And then almost indistinguishable from all the other images on their feed, you'll usually find a hashtag #ad at the end of the captions.

With that slight difference on the post, you get a glimpse on how influencers are monetizing their influence on Instagram or any other social platform. And by monetization, I'm talking as high as six-figure income earners on Instagram. Some Instagrammers can demand $20,000 for a single post, and the crazy thing is, companies are more than willing to pay these hefty fees.

As it turns out, being an influencer isn't a constant vacation. For many of these social media influencers, it's a full-time job. These men and women consider themselves to be social media influencers and marketing professionals who are helping transform traditional marketing and advertising.

Now I know what you might be thinking. How in the world do I get to 88,000 followers on social media when I've barely begun?

Well, it's good to mention here that most of the social media rockstars your see, whether they are Instagrammers or YouTubers started working on their accounts while in high school. It often begins as a hobby posting images around fashion, beauty, video games and other products.

And they are involved in this for years before they ever become highly paid influencers with hundreds of thousands of followers. But you don't need to have such a massive following to monetize your online influence, and it doesn't even matter if you're just starting out.

If you get thrilled anytime you think of yourself as a social media influencer sharing your passion with the world, then you're definitely the right fit for this book. You'll learn how to build your personal brand and a captivated audience, so that big brands can start paying you to post online.

In our digitally connected world where more time is spent online interacting with various types of content and engaging in conversations, savvy individuals are spotting an opportunity of a lifetime. Have you?

Chances are you've acquired this book because you're already aware of the emerging opportunity to design a lifestyle business that richly rewards you and enables you to do more of the things you love.

A few years ago I started noticing a significant shift on platforms like YouTube and Facebook. Everyday people were building large communities, creating content and attracting significant opportunities from well-known brands, which turned into lucrative deals. When Instagram came along, I didn't pay much attention to it. As a regular blogger (though it was still a hobby at the time), I made the mistake of underestimating the significant trend that Instagram would start, and although it took me a while, I quickly caught on.

I have watched as me, and my friends go from zero followers on Instagram to making $15,000 a month within the first year of growing our lifestyle brands and although I'm not here to make any claims, I am confident that the strategies I'm about to share with you could very well take you from an unknown person to a social media influencer in a matter of months.

Of course, that actual result is entirely dependent on your commitment, efforts, and ability to implement these proven strategies.

What started out as a hobby for me has turned out to be a life-changing experience, and I hope that as you go through this book, you too, will begin to see the unexplored potential in your life that's just waiting to be unleashed into the world.

When it comes to owning your life, creating your own economy and living life on your own terms, no path could be better and more enjoyable than that of building a personal brand and becoming a social media influencer.

Big brand and fortune 500 companies are desperate to pour some of their marketing budgets on influencers who have done the work and built out responsive, highly engaged tribes. And I know for a fact that your interest, curiosity or desire to become as successful as some of the people you've seen either while swiping through Instagram or binge-watching on YouTube is the main reason you picked up this book. So I don't want to waste any more time, let's cut to the chase and help you learn the ropes that will get you a lucrative online brand.

Before you can figure out "the how" it's always prudent to understand "the what." So let's start with the what.

This book is divided into sections to make your learning experience practical and easy to navigate. After perusing so many books on this topic, I realized most of them were totally confusing and overwhelming. I don't want you to feel confused or overwhelmed. That's why every section is jam-packed with simple, easy to follow strategies.

I do however recommend you go through it in the order presented if you wish to get the most out of it. In section one as I said, we focus on the fundamentals. Understanding what you're getting into when you decide to become an influencer.

In section two we talk about the strategies, planning and how to build your community of delighted and engaged followers. We also talk about the power of creating world-class content and why you need to prioritize that.

In section three we talk about packaging and marketing your brand, as well as the difference between marketing and advertising that so many people trip over. I also share some valuable tips and guidelines to help you stay on the right side of the law especially as your business starts growing.

In section four we do a deep dive into the various platforms that you can establish yourself as an influencer as well as how to set them up the right way. I literally break down each of the leading platforms, I tell you how each of them works and how to make them work for you.

By the time we get to the last chapter of this section, the only thing you'll need is the step-by-step framework you can deploy immediately (which I provide in chapter nine) so that you can build your brand and become an influencer within the next few months.

But wait; let's not get ahead of ourselves here. We need to warm up the engine first in preparation for takeoff. And the best way to accomplish that is by answering two simple questions: What is a personal brand and why do you need a personal brand if you want to become a social media influencer?

What Is Personal Branding?

My mom likes to tell a story from my childhood about my obsession with soda. So embarrassing, but I'll still share it with you anyway. When I was a toddler, and we were taking a trip to the store or a friend's house, they would put me in the backseat of our Toyota in a child's car seat. As we drove down the highway, I would see ads or signposts with a lot of red and a bottle of some kind, and I would yell, "Cola!"

Now, I was only about three years old at the time, so I could barely read, but I had learned to pronounce the word "soda" and "Cola." Each time something reminded me of the red patterns on the Coke bottle, I would yell out loud in excitement hoping my mom would let me have some. I learned at a very young age to associate Coca-Cola and the taste of soda (as well as the sugar rush which I obviously loved) with the color red.

That is the power of branding.

Nike, Airbnb, Coca Cola, Ferrari, Amazon, and Apple. These are just a few business brand names that are recognized worldwide. You undoubtedly know these brands and understand the concept of a business brand.

Chances are, you're also familiar with names such as Beyoncé, The Kardashians, Tiger Woods, Richard Branson, and Oprah, just to name a few. Whatever your biases and personal opinions might be of these individuals, there's no denying you've heard of some or all of these names. They are a classic example of what we call a personal brand.

In our new digital age and the emergence of smartphones and social media, the typical personal brand has gotten a makeover. Personal branding was usually associated with celebrities and the rich and famous. Not anymore.
Things are shifting, personal branding is evolving and thanks to the power of peer-to-peer engagement through mobile devices, personal branding has expanded to include more than just blue-collar children and multimillion-dollar businesses or celebrities.

I am sure you've already been sensing this shift. Even if at first it may seem unusual to most people, the concept of personal branding especially when it comes to social media and influencer marketing requires a dynamic definition. That's why before establishing yourself as an influencer I recommend polishing your personal brand.

The simplest definition of a personal brand that I can give you is this:
Your personal brand is the combination of your skills, experiences, achievements, actions, personality and all the content you share within a given community, industry or the

marketplace both online and offline. It's the representation of who you are and the impression others perceive.

In today's world, people start by Googling your name to figure out who you are. They make an assumption of you based on what they find online whether the information is accurate or not.

It makes sense then, to polish up and deliberately work on building a personal brand that is congruent with how you want the world to perceive you as well as the products you sell. Personal branding, therefore, becomes the consistent and intentional process of creating an important public perception, so that you can be viewed as an authority and someone who is credible enough to be trusted.

Why Build A Personal Brand?

Perception is everything in today's world. Deliberately building a personal brand as you grow your influencer business gives you the opportunity to make sure others perceive you in the most beneficial way. It gives you control over your self-image as well as your overall brand and enables you to highlight your strengths and passions.

The more authentic you can be across the board, the easier it will be for people to trust you and as we all know, influencer marketing is ultimately about building a community that believes in you. When people feel like they know, like and trust you (even if they never met you in person), they are more likely to buy whatever you have to offer.

If you want to become influential, you need a strong personal brand. There's just no shortcutting this part of your business growth. And the best part about working on your personal brand is that it helps you stand out from the crowd. No one else can be you, so when you learn how to integrate that uniqueness into your business strategically, you become one-of-a-kind and memorable.

As millennials continue to gain more spending power, their distrust of traditional marketing and advertising continues to grow. Research has shown that 84% of millennials have a hard time trusting both big brands and the dry advertisements they create. But this same group is prepared to believe people they feel like they "know."

As a result of this shift in consumer behavior, businesses have to rethink how they market and advertise. In fact, the main reason influencer marketing has become so huge in the last couple of years is due to this movement towards connection with a real person in a business rather than an impersonal brand.

Of course, when the business is small, it's easier to make the shift. For bigger companies, however, it has become a significant challenge that they are hoping to overcome by the use of influencer marketing. I assume that's the gap you intend to fill with your business as a social media influencer? If yes, then take the time to self-reflect, introspect and thoughtfully design your personal brand from a foundation of knowing yourself.

Your personal brand needs to match your values, mission, and purpose as well as your targeted clientele. It's about consciously building up your reputation in a way that aligns with the area of expertise you wish to become known for.

Think for a moment of a well-known figure in the adult entertainment industry - Hugh Hefner.

Hefner had a personal brand long before the term even existed, and he's lived out his entire life portraying the lifestyle a true playboy would have. He gave his readers a matching image to what he was selling thus enhancing his Playboy empire in a very congruent way. His readers have continued to be loyal to the brand because he represents it accordingly.

You want your brand and everything else you do to be just as congruent and relatable to your potential and existing clients. The more you do this, the faster your influence will grow.

Chapter 02: Influencer Marketing

Influencer marketing is the name we've given to a hybrid process that integrates old and new marketing tools and techniques. It takes the idea of the celebrity endorsement and places it into a modern-day content-driven marketing campaign.

The main difference, however, is that influencer marketing is about developing genuine relationships. Unlike celebrity endorsements, which were usually superficial and purely transactional arrangements, influencer marketing helps both the brand and the influencer. As the influencer helps create greater visibility for a brand's product or service, the influencer better serves his or her audience, grows a new enriching relationship with the brand being promoted and the brand, in turn, increases its reach and potential sales.

As more people continue to use the Internet, shopping online is becoming a standard way of life. The impact of traditional media is continuing to wear off because, at the end of the day, it's about getting consumer attention. And in today's market, attention is online, especially on social platforms. This, in short, is the reason behind the growing industry commonly referred to as influencer marketing. Simply stated, those with large, engaged audiences now possess more power than most traditional media.

As more prominent brands recognize this trend, they are choosing to invest their marketing and advertising dollars on said individuals and truth be told, it is a wise investment because consumers today are more interested in personalization.

According to Wikipedia, Influencer marketing also known as influence marketing is a form of marketing in which focus is placed on influential people rather than the target market as a whole on social media. In other words, it's about identifying savvy individuals who have influence over a specific group on potential customers online and crafting marketing activities around these influences.

Influencer marketing derives its value from three core sources:

Original content: This is where you as an influencer create unique, engaging content. The content needs to be useful, purposeful and it needs to be a mix of information that grows your brand as well as the brands you choose to promote.

Consumer trust: This is where you build and maintain strong relationships with your carefully cultivated audience. Your audience is the key to your success. It's your job to win the trust of your audience (tribe as I like to call it) because the more they trust and feel connected to you, the more they will value your opinion and anything you have to sell.

Social reach: This is your ability to reach millions of consumers through your social channels and blogging platform.

What makes an influencer

To give a firm and rigid answer to this question is to limit a very dynamic industry. No one-liner can fully identify what an influencer is or what makes one. There are always varying factors that lead to one becoming an influencer, and if you ask 10 different experts what it takes to become an influencer, you'll come out with 10 different answers. One thing is certain, however. Influencer marketing depends mainly on the context and the medium of influence communication whether that is online, offline or both.

An influencer can be a buyer, or he or she may be a third party existing either in the supply chain as a retailer, manufacturer, etc. Or they could be value-adding influencers such as academics, industry analysts, journalists, and professional advisers.

As a paid influencer you receive a product, service or experience, either for free or heavily discounted with the final goal that you will use your networking skills and social media following to spread good vibes about that particular product or service with the ultimate aim of generating more business for the brand.

Can anyone become an influencer?

Due to the fact that influencer marketing revolves around ordinary everyday people with a captivated audience, I am convinced that anyone anywhere can become a social media influencer. But perhaps not everyone should. It takes a certain level of commitment, planning, and persistence to really succeed in this industry. One must develop a thick skin and come from a mindset of abundance and collaboration; otherwise, things could get really ugly.

More importantly, you really need to be passionate about becoming an influencer and have a drive that enables you to keep going even when things get tough and trust me, they will!

The journey ahead is full of obstacles and naysayers. Getting people to follow and believe in your ideas doesn't come easy, so you need to be sure this is what you want to do with your life at least for the next couple of years. If it does feel like the path you need to be on, then help make the journey a bit more pleasant by avoiding these rookie mistakes that many newbies get caught up in.

Mistakes to avoid if you want to succeed as a social media influencer

As with any business, if you want to succeed as a social media influencer, there are certain pitfalls you're better off avoiding as you construct your campaigns and grow your brand. The more aware you are of certain blind spots that usually destroy success in this industry, the better equipped you will be as you grow and scale your business. Here are a few.

Mistake #1: Buying your followers

This has to be one of the worst mistakes an aspiring social media influencer could make. And yet so many still do. First of all, you should know that social platforms would punish you greatly if you buy followers.

For example, Greg Jones experienced firsthand how unforgiving Instagram is when he made this grievous mistake of giving his account a little boost. He felt he wasn't growing fast enough.

After a year of daily posting and engagement, he only had a little over 5,000 followers. He figured it would take too long to get to 100,000 (which was his goal). And so he bought some followers and overnight went from under 10,000 to over 100,000 followers. Soon after that, his account was forcibly shut down. Ouch!

If you are serious about being an influencer, play the long game and don't let anyone convince you that any good can possibly come from buying followers. Avoid this mistake like the plague itself!

Mistake #2: Focusing only on follower counts

Oftentimes big brands and companies will target a social media influencer based on their follower count. The larger the number, the easier it becomes to get paid... Or so it used to be!

It's easy to conclude that the more followers you have, the better, but this isn't the case anymore. I'm not saying follower count doesn't matter, but it's not the only factor to take into account nowadays. Recently, all social media platforms including Instagram have upgraded their systems providing us with the capability to measure more metrics, and companies are becoming aware that followership doesn't equal engagement or responsiveness.

In the chapter on platforms, you'll learn how to set up your account the right way on these social platforms so you can have access to the necessary insights and metrics.

If your audience is unresponsive to your content, it doesn't matter how large the number is, you won't be in a position to charge high fees or get the job done well for your clients. Don't overlook the power of engagement as you build your tribe. Sometimes a smaller following can be just as lucrative for you and the brands you work with.

Mistake #3: Staring with no proper planning

You must have a precise and detailed plan if you want to succeed in this industry. Strategy at every phase is essential. You need to have a business plan, a branding document, a documented content strategy plan, a content plan, and editorial calendar, a content inventory strategy and you also need a framework that helps you serve brands that want to hire you.

Clarity is everything when starting out and it will ensure you build a solid business so don't skip over the planning and strategizing phase of your business development.

Mistake #4: Getting into it for the money

This is a common one especially for so-called "fitness influencers." They hear the money is good and get excited about the thought of becoming an online celebrity so rather than building a client-focused business, they focus on what's in it for them.

This is the best way to dip yourself into imminent failure. Whatever recognition or social fame you manage to gather will be very fleeting if you're just "using" your community to make money and become famous. There's no easy way to say this to you, but if money is your biggest priority, find other ways of acquiring it that doesn't involve taking advantage of this human need for "love and belonging" which is what a community is meant to be.

Mistake #5: Relying on Bots

If patience, persistence, and hard work don't come naturally to you, this industry will probably not yield much profit long term. Influencer marketing is always about playing the long game.

Equally as bad as buying followers is using bots to grow your community. Relying on bots to do the work for you essentially makes you a cheater. Bots can never substitute the real and raw human interaction necessary to build a true community.

Growing a strong follower count that positions you as an expert and influencer is laborious but that is indeed the only way you'll be able to monetize your role as an influencer.

Mistake #6: Replying to comments slowly or not at all

As I said before, there is great power in engagement within your tribe. The more people share, comment and interact with your content the higher you rank on Google as well as in the eyes of brands that are looking for influencers in your space.

You can only get people to interact by demonstrating that you care about each and every individual on your list, especially in the beginning. You must reply promptly to the comments people leave you even if it's a simple thank you for a simple compliment. Encourage conversations by asking your followers a question in your captions or posts.

Respond even when it's uncomfortable for you or if someone doesn't react the way you'd hoped. Remember all feedback is valuable. These small actions on your end go a long way to show your followers that you genuinely care about them and their opinions.

Now that you know which pitfalls to avoid, you're on the right path to setting up and growing a community and business that will attract big brand opportunities. Before jumping into the strategy sections, let's make sure we have clarity on the business you wish to have.

Start with the end in mind

If you enjoy spending time on social media platforms and feel passionate about a particular topic or niche, then you'll definitely enjoy the perks of being an influence. However, this business still requires the same structure and planning as would any other. And the best place to begin is always with the end in mind as Stephen Covey taught in his book.

The fact that you will spend most of your time interacting with people, trying to influence their behavior, thoughts, opinions and even purchase decisions means you need to know what motivates you. You can only show up as your best version to serve a growing audience when you understand your motivations, objectives and who you are.

Invest some time at this phase of your business to paint a clear vision of what you ultimately want to experience as an influencer. You need to understand your core values, the priorities that matter to you, the purpose behind your business and the mission you will serve. The more clarity you have on this end picture, the easier it becomes to design a lifestyle and business you'll love.

Practical exercise:

Here are some questions to self-reflect upon. Take a journal or notebook and answer each one with as much detail as you can before moving on to section two.

1. What are my core values?

2. What is my life vision?

3. What am I passionate about or very interested in?

4. What are my superpowers (the things I do better than everyone I know)?

5. What are 5 words that describe me?

6. What is my story?

7. What most strongly sets me apart from my peers?

8. What issue/problem am I trying to solve?

9. Why does resolving this problem matter to me?

10. What is my most prominent belief about myself?

11. What are my strengths, weaknesses and current opportunities that I need to become aware of?

12. How do I represent myself?

13. Are there any changes/improvements I want to make?

14. Why am I choosing to become an influencer?

15. Why does becoming a highly paid influencer matter to me?

16. How will becoming a highly paid influencer change my life?

17. Where do I see my business going?

18. What is the biggest challenge I'm facing now?

19. What are my short-term business goals?

20. What are my long-term business goals?

21. What is the fundamental purpose behind my brand and this business I am building?

22. What mission do I want to serve through my brand?

23. What is the value I promise to deliver to my audience?

24. What is the value I promise to provide to my paying clients?

25. What are my deal breakers when it comes to accepting paid brand contracts?

26. Why should the market believe in my ideas and me?

27. Do I feel like I am the right and credible person to take on this role?

Key highlights from this section:

• Personal branding is a must for anyone who wants to become an influencer in any industry. As such you must diligently work on developing a strong personal brand online.

• Big brands and fortune 500 companies are very eager to invest in influencer marketing because they anticipate a good return on investment. In other words, they are out there looking to partner with you right now.

• Anyone can become a social media influencer today and build a large community of active members.

• To become a social media influencer requires very little capital but it does need someone with the right work ethics, a strong, abundant mindset and the heart to serve others.

• You must play the long game and think long-term if you want to become wealthy, successful and influential in your space.

• Like any business, there must be a precise strategic plan of implementation if you want this business to succeed.

• The road to success is filled with many pitfalls, many of which can be avoided with a little awareness and a real grasp of who you are and how you want to run your business.

• Getting to know who you are, what your values are, what your purpose is and the mission you will serve is a critical component of ensuring your business is established on the right foundation. So be sure to complete the practical exercise on self-reflection and self-inventory.

Section Two

"People want to do business with you because you help them get what they want. They don't do business with you to help you get what you want."

- Don Crowther

Chapter 03: Building your Tribe

Whether you realize this or not, becoming an influencer has very little to do with you and everything to do with the audience you build. People are your biggest asset. And if you're not excited about learning everything you can about the people you want to connect with, there's little hope for success in your horizon.

The business of social media influence is centered around an actively engaged community. I like to call it a tribe.

This is because when you approach your efforts in growing an audience with this nurturing mindset, you tend to make all the right moves. A tribe is more than just an audience gathering together on your page. These are your people. They resonate with your perspective and worldview, and they feel a special bond, which is all-important when it comes to selling anything.

Therefore rather than building an audience, I encourage you to focus on building a tribe of people who are passionate about what you do and can't wait to hear from you. At the end of the day, the power lies with this tribe. You can only become a superstar influencer if your tribe decides you are one and it's your job to help influence that outcome.

One of the key ideas I'd like to share with you is that your tribe doesn't just exist online. Yes, they will spend a lot of time on the social platform, but these are real people going to work, going to the gym, shopping in supermarkets and eating in restaurants. Therefore, as you build your influence, get creative. Find ways to nurture your tribe both online and offline. It may just fast track your business growth.

How to get your ideal audience to notice and fall in love with you

It's easy to get someone to fall in love with you when they feel attracted to you. It's also easy to get someone to fall in love with you when they feel seen and understood by you. Your job as an influencer is to be a valuable go-to person for your audience. You need to be that virtual friend that makes them feel like they matter and that they belong. And it begins with the content you post.

Brands want to work with an influencer who is persuasive. Someone who receives positive responses and initiates ongoing conversations within his/her tribe.

There are many ways to go about establishing such a relationship with your tribe. Start with these few and keep upgrading as you grow.

Share your story and help your tribe connect it to their own

Storytelling is the new power play in marketing and advertising. The brands that do it well shall continue to win even during the worst of times. If you learn to integrate storytelling in your business, you will stand out authentically and win.

Storytelling really helps you connect with your audience. My recommendation is that you create a story brand script that allows your tribe to connect your story with their own journey.

Consider all the great movies that you've ever watched and loved. The thing that hooked you and made it so memorable was the fact that you could relate. You experienced the character's story as your own. That's what you want to help your tribe experience as much as possible.

Human beings in today's digitally connected world have an attention span that is shorter than a goldfish according to expert reports. And retaining mundane data or information is always hard for an average person so if you want to stand out use storytelling to connect your brand, and the products you represent to your growing tribe.

Get Creative
Social media platforms are crowded, and there are a lot of influencers trying to capture the attention of your audience. You need to be original as well as highly creative. Figure out ways to get creative so you can get more attention.

Try different features on your chosen platforms as well. Now that most platforms offer several features incorporate all of them as much as you can to see which one gets your followers more fired up and excited.

Lead with your passion

Connect your tribe with your ideas, desires and the mission you serve. If you are an activist for something or an expert educator in a particular field, share this information with your growing tribe. Help them understand your "WHY" and if you do a good job tying it in with their interests, it will create a strong bond.

A community is built and sustained not by logos and fancy graphics but by shared beliefs and ideas.

Create, quality, engaging content consistently

Although we are going to dive deeper into the importance of content creation in chapter four, this is one of the critical aspects of growing your tribe that must be mentioned here. Your content will become the introduction your audience experiences so you must do your research right. Figure out which types of content work best across each platform for the tribe you wish to nurture. Make sure it's high-quality content. The more people believe in your content, the higher your chances of growing an influential brand.

Publish this content consistently, diligently do your research and make sure you produce killer content that can be repurposed across many channels. Then allow yourself to be adaptable across each platform.

Stay relevant and true to your topic

In today's digital landscape, it doesn't matter how many times a day you post as long as what you post is relevant and engaging. If you're the type of influencer who continuously posts unrelated, self-promotional products people will consider you spammy, and you'll lose.

As much as it does help to publish lots of content regularly in this line of work, quality matters more, and it's important you realize that social media content needs to have an intended audience, purpose, and goal.

Your social feed shouldn't be cluttered and filled with spammy information. It needs to have a clear message that appeals to a specific niche. Your aesthetics, framing and messaging needs to be true to you and in resonance with the audience receiving it. The more you hit that sweet spot, the more your audience will engage and continue to follow you.

Finding a sustainable interest or passion

Do you know why most social media influencers start out strong only to hit a brick wall? Or why so many still make little to nothing for their hard efforts even though Forbes reports that an influencer with 100,000 followers can easily earn around $5,000 for a single post?

The main reason is that influencers skip over the critical step of finding a niche that suits their interest. In the next few minutes, I'm going to be helping you narrow down your focus, figure out your topic or niche and establish your authentic voice. But before we do, here's a simple example of what you must never do.

Stephanie Shukle is aspiring to become a social media influencer. When we first met for our consultation session, I quickly realized she had chosen a niche (weight loss for brides) not because she was passionate or even interested in brides but because she'd heard there was lots of money to be made.

This is the fast route to never making it as an influencer. It wasn't sustainable; she wouldn't enjoy consistently creating high-quality original content, or investing countless hours and late nights working on getting the attention of brides hanging out online. Yet she was willing to do it for the money. After taking her through the series of self-reflective questions I gave you in section one (I assume you answered every question too), it was clear this wouldn't be a self-sustaining interest.

The critical takeaway lesson here is to find the alignment between your chosen niche and what you're passionate or at least interested in. You'll devote a lot of time; sweat equity, resources and money into growing this business so it might as well be something you're interested in. To be a successful influencer long term, make sure you choose the niche that most interests you, which also has a large enough audience that consumer brands will be interested in targeting.

Establishing clarity in your voice and finding your niche

Choosing your niche and developing a clear voice go hand in hand. I know they can seem daunting and tough to navigate when you're building your brand, but I will try to simplify the process as much as possible.

After all, the last thing you want is to build a brand that you can't stand!

Although it's easy to look at people like Tony Robbins and Gary Vee and think they became who they are through mere strategy, the truth is, they have evolved over time. You just need to look at their first videos to see what I mean. Their "voice" has matured and changed over time to match the demands of their audience, and in turn, they've become very profitable.

I think it's pointless to stress too much over finding your place and your voice in your space.

You start where you are with what you've got. Do the best you can to be true to yourself and keep evolving as you grow with the business.

All you need to do especially, in the beginning, is just speak about your subject matter in an intelligent and inspiring way. As a natural consequence, your voice will unfold. Test things out as much as you can and learn from the feedback you receive. At the end of the day, your audience and the marketplace are what shape the way you talk about your topic (your voice) and the more you stay open to hearing what people truly want from you, the easier it will be to refine how you get your message across to produce the outcome you most desire.

When it comes to finding your space and picking your niche, specialization is key. So make sure you do some due diligence and answer the following questions before taking that leap of faith.

Practical exercise:

Pick up your journal once again and let's do a little actual training.

1. What are you passionate about?

Get more detailed here. If you're not sure about your passions, then write down the things you find interesting enough. When you don't like dealing with the subject matter or the people in your industry for extended hours daily, you won't have the drive needed to push through tough times as you rise to success.

2. Are there other buyers interested in my niche?
This is where research begins. It's essential to research on your topic because you want to make sure there's a market for your niche and that people are spending money.

If you pick something that's too small or where buyers don't exist it's going to be tough getting brands to work with you because they won't see the ROI of the partnership. Using Google Trends, Facebook, Instagram and other social platforms you can be able to determine whether your chosen niche works.

3. Are there other influencers in my niche?
Contrary to what you might have heard growing up, competition is a good thing. You want to know that there is someone in your space doing something similar to what you want to do and they are crushing it already. And when you seek out influencers, aim for people who are already where you desire to be.

4. How will I monetize my niche?
While I have gone deeper into the monetization of your influencer business in another book, let me share a few insights here. Carve out a clear path to the money in the niche you've chosen. Make sure there are both buyers and sellers of products and services that appeal to you. Do some due diligence on the brands that are active in your niche and figure out the channels and methodologies these brands are using to communicate with their customers.

The more clarity you gain as you answer these questions, the clearer your voice will be. Sharing a consistent message across all your platforms will be easy.

Choosing your message

It's time to bring out your whiteboard and sticky notes. Everything about this next phase will be work in progress, but you must start from somewhere. Never assume that once you define your message, everything else is done.

In your line of work, everything depends on the feedback you get from the audience, which means it will be a constant process of reiteration from the first message you decide to use. Once you put yourself out there and start sharing your message, get feedback and data to see how the clients respond, and then make the necessary adjustments to your brand's messaging.

Practical exercise:

1. Start by defining what makes your brand unique or different.
It needs to be something valuable to your customers, and it must articulate aspects of your business that cost you something to uphold.

Come up with 5 -10 key differentiators and write some supporting details for the ones that stick out. Then finally chose one of these to use as your main statement of reference for now.

2. Develop your one-liner
Also called a tagline. It should capture the essence of what you and your brand represents and how you serve your customer. Take into account your core values, mission statement and the differentiation statement you just created in section one. Write down 10-20 one-liners at a minimum. You may find that you end up going down a creative path with one particular idea or word so cluster those ones into the same group.

In the end, you might have 4 or more clusters with many one-liners. Just let these ideas flow without judgment. There is no right or wrong. In the end, you will find one that stands out and meets all the criterion often associated with awesome taglines.

An example of this would be from Apple: Think Different. Ideally, your one-liner should be memorable, intriguing, and unique to your brand and personality and it shouldn't be more than a sentence. If you can't decide on the perfect fit, survey your friends or even your growing audience and let them participate as you grow your brand.

3. Create your elevator pitch

As much as people think being a social media influencer is about taking selfies and messing around lazily on social feeds throughout the day, this is a real business that requires real strategy and frameworks.

Moreover, to become a highly paid influencer requires you to connect with brands that are willing and looking to work with an influencer. When that opportunity presents itself, you need to be ready and equipped. That's where your elevator pitch comes in.

You need to have a strong elevator pitch so that you can easily communicate your brand to those who don't know you in the shortest time frame possible without losing their attention. The reason it's called an elevator pitch is that it should essentially be communicated in the brief amount of time it takes to go up a few floors in an elevator.

When giving your elevator pitch to strangers and potential brands that you want to work with, make sure you inspire the person enough desire more information. Explain what you do in a tone that gives the person an idea of what it's like to work with you or be in your world. Below I share the key things your elevator pitch needs to have to generate a reaction that will please you.

• Start with your "who."
Get to know who makes up your audience. Do you have moms? Dads? Teens? Vegans?
The more you know about your audience, the easier it will be to identify a potential brand that would be interested in working with you. Check your Google Analytics and Social Media insights to know more about your audience and their behavioral patterns. You can learn the age range, gender and location from all the major social platforms when you have a business account. But don't stop there. You need to know the psychographics of your audience as well.

Let's assume your audience is dads. What are their hobbies? What other influencers or magazines or books do they follow? Where do they mostly like to hang out online?

Of course, getting such details is tougher if you're just relying on analytics so strategically engage and interact more with your audience. The more time you spend directly conversing with your audience, the better you'll know them.

One of the best ways to do this live interaction is through live video streams. Aside from the fact that Facebook, Instagram, and LinkedIn are pushing out video content above all others (which means you'll get more reach), people enjoy consuming video content. Through Facebook Live, Instagram Live or Instagram Stories, your audience will get the opportunity to decide if they genuinely like you and your brand. It also gives you the chance to know more about them.

If you also have a list already built, that's another excellent way to discover more about your audience. Share more of your personal stories and relate them back to your mission and brand. Ask questions and encourage direct responses so that your audience can feel comfortable enough sharing their stories as well. Regardless of the channels you use, make sure you prioritize knowing as much as you can about your audience before going to pitch potential brands.

• Figure out the pain point and the solution:
Once you know your audience, it's time to hone your message. More specifically - what solution do you have for the brands you want to work with?

Your audience has a pain point or problem that they feel you help solve or remedy. Do you have clarity on what that is? It could be something as simple as knowing which baby bottle brand to get for their newborn or which perfume to buy for Valentines. It could be what types of clothes a man should wear to improve their personal appearance and increase self-confidence.

Whatever your audience routinely comes to you for, will become an opportunity for you to collaborate with brands because when a brand realizes that you can influence people to purchase a particular product, they will be very eager to work with you.

Again, going back to analytics and using data to inform us on our pitch, we can be able to track the content that performs the best. At times we might think our audience comes to us for one thing only to discover they care more about a topic we didn't even think was relevant. For example, if you're an influencer sharing content around healthy vegetarian food, you might think people come to you for healthy tips, but when you go through the backend data, you realize they actually come to you for comforting vegetarian recipes. By gaining this realization, you're better equipped to identify the problem that you actually solve, and it empowers you to attract more of your ideal audience as well as relevant brands.

• Test to make sure the elevator pitch makes sense and answers the right question satisfactorily:

For this to work, you'll need some practice. Pause for a moment and imagine you're standing in an elevator with the CEO of a cool brand you'd love to work with.

He asks you, what is it you do?

What would be your answer to that? You want to make sure the elevator pitch you create is a perfect statement answering that question. As you craft, your elevator pitch think from the question, incorporate the various aspects I've outlined in this entire chapter and make sure you compress it into something short, concise and straightforward enough for this CEO to get before he jumps off the elevator.

If you can do this right, you'll not only create a killer elevator pitch, but you'll also gain real followers fast!

4. Have a stunning bio and "about me" page

The more people can clearly understand who you are and what you do, the easier it will be to attract the right audience and the right brands. That means you need to have your bio in all relevant places online. Even if you don't have a website, you can use sites like Wix and About Me.com to set up a professional bio that dives deep into who you are and what you do.

Crafting your message

If your message doesn't resonate with your audience, it becomes really tough to grow as an influencer and attract high paying brands. In today's noisy world, finding your message and making sure your audience shares the same view is critical.

Don't be confused by this idea of honing down your messaging. At this point I am not referring to your brand identity (that can come later), I am focusing purely on what matters to your audience. You can only find your message when you understand what your audience truly cares about and then tie it in with your brand's mission and values.

There's massive competition in the world of social media influencing. It's not enough to hang your hat and post a few selfies every day. You need to actually stand out from the crowd and become recognized for a particular topic. Maximize Social Business suggests that there are around eight million active "mommy bloggers" in the world. Can you imagine how competitive that area must be if you want to stand out?

You'd need to have a pretty loud voice to heard. But then again, being the loudest online doesn't necessarily mean you'll do well. People might just tag you as noisy or spammy especially if you're also promoting brands and products.

Regardless of your chosen niche, if it's a thriving market, there's bound to be plenty of competition. So rather than trying to be a loud mouth why not focus all your energy on honing down your niche and messaging?

After all, the smart brands and marketers looking to work with influencers today aren't necessarily looking for social influencers with massive followings (although it does help); they are looking for influencers with a tribe that is active and motivated.

What this means for you (especially if you have a small to medium sized tribe) is that as long as you can pick a subject matter and gain a vast amount of knowledge and credibility on it within your tribe, brands will start flocking to you.

Crafting the right message is about testing.

As hard as this might be to grasp, your tribe doesn't really care about you or your goals. They care about the things that matter to them. Often what your brand values won't matter to the audience you're trying to grow. That's why you need to craft your message through a series of test experiments where you ask your community what problems they face. Then it's up to you to figure out how to help them solve those problems.

If you do this right, you'll find you have more than 10 different messages or solutions. Start with choosing two that really excite you and come up with various strategies for communicating each one. Videos, blog posts, testimonials, success stories, pictures are all great ways of expressing your message.

From there, run tests to see which message and method gain more traction in the growing community. The more you learn what your tribe cares about, the greater impact and scale your messaging will have.

It will also make it easier for the brands that are a perfect fit for you to spot you. This level of clarity makes creating your pitch easy too, and we all know when the focus is placed on delivering what the audience wants, selling happens naturally.

Remember not every message you try will work. You might end up creating and testing 20 messages before you find one that hits a home run. The important thing is to keep testing and be mindful of the fact that tweaking is necessary when moving from one platform to the next. The same message that works well on Facebook may not do as well on Twitter. Learn to adjust accordingly. Once you've crafted a message that represents your brand well and aligns with your audience, you're ready to start selling products and services that resonate with your tribe.

Chapter 04: The Magic Of Great Content Creation

Original high-quality content is a crucial aspect of any successful influencer business. It is a core tool for your entire business. That's why you need to take the necessary measure to ensure your content is successful and trustworthy.

In this chapter, we dive into different aspects of content creation and how to set yourself up for success. But before that, let's draw a line in the sand here so you can stop making the grievous mistake of comparing yourself to influencers who are walking a different path. You see not all influencers are the same and it's time you make your stand.

Two kinds of online influencers, which side will you pick?

A twenty-two-year-old posted on her Instagram feed an image of herself and one of the Kardashian twins. You know the one who is super famous on Instagram? And on her captions she asked in disappointment - how is it that I'm still not as famous as the Kardashians after 2 years of daily posting?

It's easy for an outsider like me to get judgmental and call her silly. But in truth, the girl is just misinformed. She still doesn't realize what I am about to teach you. There are two main classes of influencers online today.

The first group is the one I call celebrity influencers. These are the Mega influencers with over a million followers. The Kardashians are a good example. People just want to follow them everywhere and see what they eat, where they sleep etc. They are famous for being famous. Whether or not they post something meaningful and inspiring people continue to flock around them. Actors, athletes like Cristiano Ronaldo, artists and other social media superstars with the highest reach on the influencer spectrum also fall into this category. Their influencer is driven by their celebrity status. When it comes to resonance and driving actions on behalf of a brand, they are actually scoring the lowest in terms of return on investment. So before you start getting jealous of a Kardashian and the fact that you have no way of getting a million followers, let's look at your other option.

The second group is the one I call content creating influencers. These are often macro-influencers. They are usually self-made individuals who produce amazing content consistently that's high quality and over time build a following. Think of people like Gary Vee and Tai Lopez if you really want an example. They've chosen certain subject matters and consistently push out inspiring, educative, entertaining and motivational content causing people to flock around them too. A journalist is also a content producer, and so is a blogger, analyst, author, etc. Macro-influencers usually have between 10,000 - 1 million followers and drive 5% - 25% engagement per post. They have the highest topical relevance on the spectrum and tend to be super niched down in categories like fashion, business, and lifestyle.

Hidden within this group of influencers is a smaller subset that is quickly gaining recognition as "micro-influencers."

A micro-influencer is like a mini version of a macro-influencer. Usually, these individuals are everyday consumers or employees who have between 500 - 10,000 followers and they actually have the highest brand relevance and resonance on the spectrum of influencers believe it or not. A micro influencer drives 25%-50% engagement per post, and because personal experience and relationship building within their networks drive their influence, they are quickly becoming some of the highest paid influencers.

The question is which side do you want to be on?

While anyone can produce content, not everyone can create amazing content that turns him or her into an influencer at whatever scale. Influential content is widely read, liked, commented on and shared. As a content creator, you don't need to have a large tribe to do well. What you need is to be seen as a credible authority on that topic and somewhat of an expert. You also need to be relatable. Many beauty influencers are relatable girls who consistently keep their audiences entertained, informed and inspired. So if like that twenty-two-year-old girl you're frustrated by the lack of fame, stop and re-assess your goals. Make a definite decision on whether you want to be on the side of mega influencers (the painful path to success) or on the side of macro and micro influencers.

Keep in mind that people like the Kardashians have a more massive empire they are building as a family all managed by their mom who is the key behind it all. And you're probably just a one man or one-woman show starting from scratch. The fame might eventually come, but don't waste your energy on wishful thinking. Pick a side that you know is the level ground where you can utilize all the resources available to you and create a meaningful community.

Aside from knowing where you stand as an influencer, it's also important to be strategic about this content you're creating. It's great that you're determined to put out world-class content, but how will you manage it all?

How will you ensure you're always consistent, on time and in alignment with your brand identity and messaging? The simple solution is to document your content strategy.

Documenting your content strategy

Your content strategy can be a few pages long or the size of a small book. It all depends on how detailed you want to be. But there's no escaping the fact that if you truly want to run a successful business, you need one. A documented strategy will help guide your decision-making. It will make it easier for you to visualize your entire ecosystem. It will also keep you accountable as you go through the planning, scheduling, publishing, and distribution of the actual content.

Many moving parts make up a content strategy, and it should be crafted around your specific needs and objectives. I encourage you not to abide by a rigid template. So rather than attempt to give you a one size fits all, let me outline what your document should include and then you can build upon and customize it to meet your needs.

• Current state
Make an assessment of your existing content as well as some insights into your competitor's content. Include the following:
Personas
Content Inventory
Competitive analysis
Gap analysis
Content audit

• Future of your content

This is where you gain clarity on where you want your content to take you and the various channels you will use to get there. Some of these places include:

Onsite content such as your landing pages, homepage, blog, etc.

Offsite content such as social media, emails etc.

• The content eco-system

You want to be able to create an environment in which the content is created. This also includes the way your content shall be governed adhering to your branding efforts. Some of these elements include an editorial calendar, brand voice and style guidelines as well as workflow analysis.

These steps might be a great starting point.

Step One: Document your discovery phase

This is the phase where you assess both the present and future of your content. It's where you ask yourself "why" you're doing what you're doing and the purpose this content should serve to help you express that why. After going through the various exercises in this book, it should be easy for you to identify your content objectives.

1. What task do you want the content to accomplish?

2. What behaviors do you want to influence with your content?

3. What are the goals, fears, and motivator of the audience you want to reach with your content?

4. Who are their heroes? What about their enemies?

5. Are there any content gaps that need to be filled?

6. Does your mix of channels make sense given your goals?

7. What content is currently working and what isn't?

Step Two: Document your content program

After going through step one, you should have a clear understanding of what to prioritize as you launch and feel free to tweak things as you go. This is always a continuous process. The elements that must be included in this phase are:

1. Your methodology for measuring.

This is what will inform your success at each stage of your business growth. Decide on the KPIs (Key Performance Indicators) that matter to you. Make sure they are specific, and all connect back to your goals.

2. Journey mapping

Outline the journey your leads and audience go through before they are ready to purchase something. How will your prospects be nudged along this journey? Are there signals to help you figure out which stage someone is in and can you create a particular technique to help move them along and have them ready to take action when you do make an offer? At what point will you start monetizing the audience?

3. Messaging

How is your content supporting your brand messaging? Which messages are currently relevant to the goals you want to reach? Will key messages resonate with all audiences or do you need to segment and personalize things more?

4. Channel opportunities

Take a look at all the channels and strategies you use (paid and organic) to get your audience to gather some audience insights. If you don't yet have any data, it's still worthwhile asking yourself these questions. How will you reach your audience? What will your mix of channels be?

5. Storytelling opportunities

Although many people consider this to be optional, as a social media influencer, it's crucial. Stories are what emotionally engage humans, and you need to make them a priority. You need a storytelling framework that helps you build content pillars and supports your goals.

6. SEO and Keyword planning

SEO is highly beneficial for content marketing although it's a more long-term strategy. Not all social media influencers care about SEO and keyword planning, but if you do want to use this as part of your strategy, some of the questions to answer are: How will you optimize content around keywords? What are the keywords you want to dominate? Are your publishing platforms optimized for SEO?

7.Editorial calendar

The editorial calendar will help you decide on things like, how often you will publish, how much content you'll put out daily and how you'll organize your campaigns. What formats will you create? Is your calendar aligned to the "life calendar" of your target personas? How will you publish and promote (and repurpose) each piece of content?

8. Budget Allocation

This is a huge benefit of creating a documented strategy because as you plan ahead of time, you can figure out ways of getting the most value out of your content and giving it the biggest reach. This is where the conversation on advertising comes into play. Figure out if you will use any paid ads to grow your audience and if so, work your way backward from your marketing goals to estimate the budget you'll allocate for this.

9. Outsourcing

If you need to expand and get a team, outsourcing and getting an extra hand to help complete a project might be a great way to go. In such cases, do your due diligence first to make sure you're bringing in the right creative partners and add this to your documented strategy.

10. Tools and resources

It's imperative to have the right tools to help you execute on your publishing and distribution. Although there are many bells and whistles on the web today and all kinds of software apps, you only need a handful to execute your vision well. Don't fall into the trap of buying something just because it looks good. Here are some of the resources I recommend checking out. Some are free others require monthly paid memberships.

Tools for Social media content publishing: Hootsuite and Buffer.
Platforms for blogging: Wordpress and Medium.
Tools for Analytics: Google Analytics, and Moz.
Software for Email marketing and relationship building outside social media platforms: Convertkit, Aweber, and Hubspot.

Tools for Social Monitoring: Meltwater, Trendkite

An editorial calendar and publishing tool: Coschedule

Tools for creating fast landing pages: Leadpages and Clickfunnels.

How to fuel your brand

Above and beyond creating amazing content consistently for your growing audience, you also need to find other ways of increasing your exposure. You need to find creative ways of positioning yourself as a transparent, energized influencer in the eyes of both your audience and brands looking to work with influencers. Every successful influencer needs extra fuel to keep his or her influence burning strong, and it's your job to figure out what will fuel you and your brand.

It may not be easy to push out as much content as many gurus suggest especially when just starting out and running everything on your own, but there specific creative ideas you can leverage to maximize brand reach.

One of the best ways to do this is through guest posting and creating relevant content for magazines and websites that speak on your topic. Since you're already a content creator, why not leverage your magical content by sharing it out to highly trafficked sites and magazines?

You'll get more brand recognition, build credibility and attract new people into your world. It can also open up opportunities for companies to find you or at least see your authority on your chosen niche.

You can also leverage user-generated content to continue fuelling your brand's growth and credibility. We all know that kind words from a customer are far more likely to be persuasive than your own recommendations. The more your tribe praises you, the more others will want to follow you and the more attractive you will be for high paying brands. Besides, this type of content (if published and placed in all the right places on your social channels) can continue to fuel your brand's overall content production.

Another thing to test out would be collaborations with peers in the same industry. This can be an Instagram takeover or a joint Facebook Live or any other type of collaboration where you get to be in front of a new audience, and you give your audience a chance to receive fresh new content from someone in a similar space. It also demonstrates your generosity and builds a lot of goodwill.

You and you alone are responsible for making this business work. As an influencer, you always need to have attractive, fresh content that draws more of your tribe in. You need to continually keep the fire burning by employing as many creative methods as you can conjure. Think outside the box, test out different things, and keep crafting your message and share news ideas on your chosen niche. You also need to radiate excitement in the work that you do and the tribe you're nurturing. Brands want to work with influencers who are motivated, thrilled about their products and excited to be partnering. That energy is something you learn to generate as you create and publish your own content.

Testing, testing, and more social testing

I am adding on this extra piece before jumping into the more technical aspects of growing your brand as a social media influencer because I feel it's one that few influencers learn early enough.

The world of social media marketing is dynamic, and every audience is different. What works for one tribe on a particular platform may not work on a different platform. The best advice I can give you as you start growing is to make sure you are always testing and measuring all your campaigns and social media efforts.

Don't just publish for the sake of it. As I said before, each post needs to have a purpose and tied together with that purpose is a goal that you're moving toward. Measuring your success is therefore paramount. And the more you can test different tactics and strategies out, the faster you can know what works for you. So some of the low hanging fruits that you can start testing even as a novice include:

Testing the time of day that gets you the best audience reactions. Depending on the platforms you use, test out different times. Use tools within Twitter, Facebook Instagram, and the other social platforms to figure out when your audience is most active on the platform.

Testing the posts that get the most engagement. This is also super easy to implement. When you're on Facebook, which types of images work best? Is it just a single image or two or three images? What about links?

I have actually found that using multiple images (at least 2) per post gets more engagement on my page. Now go to the other platforms and carry out this simple test.

A lot of these tests will be done manually, and it might have a learning curve, especially if you're also testing emails, landing pages, etc. But with a little practice, you'll keep getting better. As you run tests be sure only to make one change at a time. If you change multiple things at once, it will be hard to know what made things better. So for example, if you're testing for Facebook posts and you're not sure if multiple images and links work, test one at a time. First post with a change in the number of images. Use two instead of one, and leave everything else as usual. Once you figure out whether it's working or not, you can move on to testing the removal of the link.

Remember, just because you've tested an idea and found that it worked in a particular way doesn't mean that it will always work. The algorithms are ever changing on social media so yes; keep doing what works until it doesn't. Then give yourself permission to continue testing and even retesting old tactics that failed in the past. Because you never know, though it failed in the past, this time around it might just work. As long as that's the kind of attitude you have, you'll always win on social media.

Key highlights from this section:

• Instead of trying to build a following, focus on building a tribe. See your people as humans under your care and serve them from the heart. Find a way to nurture your tribe online and offline.

• Use storytelling to connect your story, the products you promote and the interests of your tribe. The more they can relate to your story and connect it with their own journey, the more relevant your brand becomes.

• Lead with your passion and interests and find a topic that you are willing to master and share with your community.

• Be creative with your content, make sure it's useful, unique and on topic. When it comes to your brand messaging, give yourself permission to let it evolve. Run tests and experimentations with the ideas you have and gain feedback and data from your tribe so you can adjust it accordingly.

• Develop a simple, concise elevator pitch for your brand using the steps outlined.

• Pick a niche that has some competition, where there are fellow influencers in the same niche and where the audience is large enough and has spending power. Otherwise, you will have a hard time getting well-paying companies to hire your brand.

• You can choose to struggle your way into stardom and hope to become a mega influencer as a result of gaining celebrity status, or you can choose to join the group of content creators and become a macro-influencer or a micro-influencer.

• To create magical content that captivates your audience, you need a plan, a lot of research and a document outlining your project so you can easily create, manage and publish content consistently.

• Leverage the tools and technology that help you organize, publish, promote and distribute your content once you go through the steps outlined in this section.

• Pick one or two tactics to increase your brand exposure. The bigger the team, the more tactics you can implement simultaneously. When starting out alone or with a small team decide on one or two, whether that's paid advertising, guest blogging or any of the other suggested ideas to make sure you are giving your brand enough exposure online.

• Test and measure all the different strategies and tactics you choose to implement in your brand. The more you do, the more you'll know what works for you and what needs improvement. This is the best way to grow and scale your business.

Section Three

" As long as I get to do my thing and someone wants to write me a check for it, I'm all about it."

- Mike Perry, Broad City Designer

Chapter 05: Packaging and Growing Your Brand

In this section, we are going to get really technical and break down uncomplicated ways you can start packaging yourself and growing your brand so that it starts becoming an income earner.

But before you can package anything, you need to have a brand identity and a growing audience. Let's talk more about that here.

A logo, a slogan, and a website are all cool, but they don't make your brand. Branding isn't something static; it's dynamic, progressive and is controlled by both you and your audience. The truth is you can do everything in your power to build your brand, but ultimately, your audience will perceive you in their mind as they choose to and there isn't much you can do about that. But what you can do is influence that perception as much as possible.

I like to think of this as helping your audience choose the right placement spot for you in their mind. To aid in this lifelong feat, there are few questions I encourage you to ask yourself as you grow and scale the business continually.

1. Who are my ideal clients (both paying and non-paying)?

2. What type of clients do I want to have?

3. What is my value proposition? Is it relevant to my audience?

4. When people think about my brand, what are the feelings and associations I want them to have?

5. What kind of personality will my brand have?

6. What are the emotional benefits that only I can deliver to my audience?

7. What brands do I admire?

8. What are my brand colors?

9. What fonts will I use in my communications?

10. How can I streamline my visual content?

11. What is my audience's "Language"?

12. What impact do I want my brand to have in the world?

How to quickly grow an engaged audience organically

While you can put some advertising budget aside to help expand your reach and brand awareness, I encourage you to focus first on organic growth. You don't want to pay for people to follow you. You can pay for more people to become aware of your content (boosting content) but let the actual following grow as a natural consequence of them discovering how amazing your content is. And since we've talked extensively about creating great content in the previous section, I'm going to assume you're ready for takeoff at this point.

I know it can get frustrating when starting out because it seems like you're just talking to yourself and no one seems interested but take comfort, we all start from there. Even the great Gary Vee said it took a lot of time to build engagement on his Twitter and YouTube channels and look at him today. I can't tell you how long it will take for you to start seeing massive participation in your community, but I can share tips that will ensure you're on the right track.

Tip #1: Incorporate a lot of video content

Videos are the most consumed type of content in today's digital world. In February 2017, Facebook CEO Mark Zuckerberg said, " I see video as a megatrend." He was so right. There's an explosion of growth in video on social media that is still predicted to continue rising. Views of branded video content increased 99% on YouTube and 258% on Facebook between 2016 and 2017 according to wyzowl. And that was just the beginning. On Twitter, a video tweet is 6X more likely to be retweeted than a photo tweet. Those are really huge numbers, and they keep growing each year.

All this to say, you need to be producing as much video content as you can.

Many of the social platforms like LinkedIn and Facebook push out video content more than other types of content and give more exposure to people who post videos regularly. If you didn't include video into your strategy, now is the time to go hard and invest heavily in video production. People like Gary Vee have built entire businesses leveraging mostly video content. You can do the same too. If you have a smartphone, you've got everything you need to get started.

Tip #2. Use hashtags often

This is a quick and essential part of quickly growing an engaged audience. It will expose your posts to new eyes and make it easier for people who don't know your brand to find and follow you. Make sure to do some research and find the right hashtags that will lead to long-term longevity. Although using a popular hashtag is a nice short-term solution, it may not always be the best idea because you might end up attracting generic people who aren't a perfect fit.

Tip #3. Engage with everyone

I've seen a lot of newbies skipping this part, and it hurts their growth. When you start posting, you need to engage with everyone who reacts to your content. It doesn't matter whether you consider them the right fit for your audience or not, if someone has taken the time to look at your content and engage, they deserve acknowledgment. Let everyone who interacts with your content know that you are human, that you care, that you are reading their responses and listening to what they want. The more people get used to this, the more they will engage whenever you post something because all humans want to be seen and heard. Use this to your brands' advantage.

Tip #4. Provide an irresistible benefit for your growing audience

Everyone is tuned into the WIIFM radio station. WIIFM (What's in it for me) broadcasts the best tunes, and when you align your brand and platform with this station, you're destined to win. People who find you online have only one question running through their minds "what's in it for me?"

If you can offer something beneficial to them right off the bat, something designed to draw them deeper into your world while at the same time adding some value in their life, you'll be building trust and a captivated audience. Come from a place of abundance. Be generous with your gift and offer something that is super relevant to the audience you're nurturing while still remaining aligned with your overall goals.

Tip #5: Gamify the process

People love to respond to quizzes and questions. Using games (if it aligns with your personality and brand style) can be a great way to grow a following quickly. You can quickly build up followers and engagement on your platform.

You and I both know being an influencer is a full-time gig that requires you to wear many different hats including content creation, photography, graphics designing, community management, and the list goes on and on. Since you're going to put this much effort into it, having an idea of how to package yourself so you can be equipped to monetize at the right time is essential.

Why do you need to consider packaging your services?

As an influencer, brands will often come to you knowing they want results, but they may not be sure how you can actually help them or worse still, they might be going in the direction that won't yield optimum results and show a high ROI, which as we know will not bode well for you. Because we know it's your reputation at stake when you chose to collaborate with a brand, it is useful to start having an idea of the different ways you can best serve the companies you want to work with.

If potential clients can see your services and how you can help them or how you've helped other brands in the past, they can start having a clear picture of the best way to collaborate with you. It's one thing for a company to make assumptions about what they need from an influencer. It's another to look at a package you've created and have them realize "yes that's exactly what we need!" Or at least pave the way for a customized service that resonates with both parties.

Therefore your job in this section is to make sure you learn to package your offers concisely and attractively for the potential companies you desire to work with. Packing your services makes it easier for your prospects to process information about you and why they should collaborate with you. It makes the decision making process easier, reduces cognitive barriers and prompts them to buy-in to your offer.

 Now it's time to decide what services you want to offer:

This can go as in-depth as you like, but I recommend starting easy. You already know the things you're passionate about, the brands that you want to work with, etc. Think along the lines of what these brands are most interested in getting across to their ideal consumers and then reverse engineer it back to you and your brand.

You might have to do some research on this and even study what other influencers in your niche are doing or check out the type of marketing the brands you wish to work with are doing.

For example, if you want to work with a sustainable clothing brand, you can create a package that includes various types of content shared across multiple platforms each tweaked to match the different social platforms so the brand can get the most out of your collaboration. You might have another packaged offer that even includes some kind of interactive educational Livestream where you take people behind the scenes and share the story of the clothing brand freshly and uniquely.

There are many ways to approach this, but the beauty of having these packages is that you can focus on offering what you absolutely love doing. That will make pouring your energy into a campaign all the more enjoyable, and those brands that resonate with your way of communicating online will quickly find you.

If there is a secret sauce to be leveraged in digital marketing, this is it!

What am I talking about?

Storytelling.

Your brand can stand out and differentiate itself easily if you integrate powerful storytelling techniques that have been proven to work. We all know the power of a great story. It's part of human nature to lean in and pay closer attention when a grand narrative is going on whether that's around a campfire, the dinner table, workshop, or over the phone. In today's world, brands like Netflix have exponentially taken over the entertainment scene because they found a way to leverage technology and place great stories in front of a hungry audience that craves uninterrupted storytelling. Creating a storybrand script that resonates with your audience and shows the human side of your business will go a long way in establishing you as a trusted expert.

Why should you focus on narratives and storytelling?

Well, first of all, it's the easiest way to make your brand relatable. Being relatable as an influencer is really important. So you need to have good relatable characters with personalities and interests. More importantly (especially for your story brand script) you need to have a common villain or conflict that unites you and your tribe.

You also need to make sure your stories have a beginning middle and an end with a pace that's easy to follow. If you open a loop, please make sure you close it before losing the attention of your audience.

Beginning - middle - end is a simple narrative arc that can be used in endless ways so let your creativity run wild as you start crafting the narratives that will help you script your brand's story and content.

There are many story scripts you can create for yourself and your brand. Be flexible with the scripts and keep testing now angles to see what generates more positive reactions.

Consider sharing what you're currently working on, or a "behind the scenes" look at what it means to be an influencer and grow a thriving business. You can also share stories about your learning experience working with brands and what that process looks like. Whatever you choose to share, make sure it's in alignment with the overall mission of the brand. Always try to stay true to your messaging and the brand image you want the world to know.

Another great tip when it comes to leveraging storytelling is to make sure the story brand script is personal, relatable and client focused. Since your clients are both paying brands and the audience you're growing, make sure they take center stage of your brand's story. When starting out, focus more on the brand's story as it relates to your audience and let things unfold naturally. People don't by into brands; they buy into the story behind the brands. You - are what people buy into and that's what makes you influential.

Reinforce your brand's message and the things you stand for. Your tribe will feel more connected the more you share these types of content on social media. For example, if you want to become an influencer in the natural health products niche and you love Whole Foods then share information that portrays that message clearly. You can share healthy tips, food recipes, and ingredients that you get from Whole Foods, etc. Perhaps you had health issues that led to this transformation, and Whole Foods played a role in helping you heal and change your eating habits. As you share that story, make sure each piece of content no matter how small is used to reinforce the story you want to communicate. As you do, your brand builds credibility and relatability. It also makes your content super relevant to a specific audience.

How to use narratives on your social platforms:

I know you might be thinking " storytelling sounds excellent and I can see that happening on my website or blog but is it efficient on social platforms?
Absolutely. Let me prove it to you by sharing a few examples on some of the social channels.

You can work narratives into your Facebook posts by turning your status updates into little blog posts. Many savvy personal brands are actually starting to do this. Authors are a great example of individuals who are regularly posting narratives on their Facebook pages. Author Anne Lammott is worth checking out. On her Facebook page, she shares stories about herself and the things that are happening around her, and it's drawing extensive comments and likes.

You can also work digital storytelling into your Instagram posts by sharing a simple narrative on your captions as you post the image. Gather inspiration from big brands like Airbnb who have mastered this art of sharing stories about each location they post. This same narrative technique can be used across almost any social network you can think of.

Can you see how simple and fun this can be if you think outside the standard way of doing things?
Most people just think about cat videos or making offers on social media. These cannot be your staple form of content if you want to stand out and actually grow.

Building a team

When is the right time for you to start building a team around your business?
There is no rigid right answer to this. Few people have the bandwidth to simultaneously cover all the necessary business areas without going insane. Whether you start off alone or with a team, you'll soon realize it takes a working team to grow a thriving business.

Many experts encourage outsourcing and putting a team together from day one. This, of course, depends a lot on your objectives, your core competencies and whether or not you have funds to support having extra people around.

In today's digital world, having a team doesn't need to be stressful and costly. If you know how to pick the right individuals, you can assemble talented freelancers and contractors who can work with you remotely. Platforms such as Upwork, Fiverr and others are great for sourcing talent. But of course, you need to be able to attract and retain the right people.

When it comes to hiring an agent, a virtual assistant and all those other roles that meant to aid you to grow and scale the business, there is also no definite time for you bring them on. But I would say these types or roles become more important for your business once you actually have an audience and some forward momentum.

Regardless of when you choose to assemble your team, you'll still need to put in the necessary work because it won't be easy. At times, building a team can be as critical and as difficult as building your brand. Finding the right team doesn't just happen overnight, and if you get a team that doesn't work well together, it doesn't matter how epic your brand is, you'll have a hard time achieving your goals.

A key take away point to include here is also about choosing your agent. Many brands and advertising companies have expressed their disappointment when having to work with an agent who doesn't represent an influencer well. If you get to a point where you choose to work with an agent, make sure they are amplifying your success not hindering it. You need someone who will represent you well in front of your paying prospects. Your agent and everyone who gains access to your paying and non-paying clients must be in alignment with your values and the core mission that you serve.

A few general pointers might go a long way in helping you envision and bring together the right people that will enable you to focus on doing more of what you love.

One. Make sure you take the time to define your business culture.
A great team begins with you. Find the right people in the different areas you need help with who resonate with you and the culture you want to nurture. It might seem like a good idea to

go for cheap or free interns and family members, but if these people aren't aligned with your thinking and vision, things will crumble pretty fast.

Two. Each team member that comes on board must choose to be proactive and contribute as best they can.
They need to fully step into their role, bring out the best in others and collaborate across their areas of expertise to deliver on the shared objective of your brand. It will be your job to measure each person's performance and results.

Three. Foster stable relationships within the team and stay focused on what matters.
If there is bad energy, lack of synergy and poor communication among the team members, it will dilute the impact and performance of the team. It's impossible for people to be productive and focus on high-quality execution when distracted by petty issues and poor relationships with one another, so I recommend clearly communicating the purpose of coming together and making sure people actually enjoy working together.

Four. Energize your team around the shared purpose of your brand, the community and what you want to achieve ultimately.
As an influencer your ability to nurture and motivate people is indispensable. That goes for the community you're growing as well as the team working in the background with you. The team can only help you build a successful social media business when the members feel appreciated, heard and valued. The more open-minded and receptive they are to your vision of the changing world and your guidance the higher your success will be. This is, therefore, no time for you to be wasting energy "protecting" yourself or "micro-managing" people because you lack faith in their ability to execute. Doing so will just dissipate the energy you could be using to build the necessary connections and bonds that lead to a successful team.

Five. Mobilize hearts and mind by converting your vision into milestones
Every new business team has a big job to do and lots of barriers, obstacles, swirling priorities, and seemingly impossible deadlines. Too many influencers make the mistake of just throwing a bunch of people together with no proper vision, clear strategy and old knowledge on how to work with others. Don't make this same mistake.

Empower your team and help them create action plans for delivering exceptional results in their assigned roles. Equip your team members with the right tools, education, and resources that enable them to ask the type of questions that lead to positive results. Let them bring innovative ideas and creativity. The more they can participate in this journey with you the more invested with will be physically, mentally and spiritually.

Assembling a team may or may not be on your immediate to do list but at some point on this journey, you will need to start forming one. When you do, keep these things in mind because getting an average team will only lead to mediocre results. You need a team that is epic to help exponentially grow and scale your brand.

Getting on the right side of the law

Even as a novice working your way up into stardom, it's essential to become aware of the rules around influencer marketing. As with any business, there are laws and regulations in place for most countries, though not all. Definitely, check in with local authorities to figure out what the law requires you to adhere to as a social media influencer.

In the United States, for example, the Federal Trade Commission (FTC) has a set of guidelines that you must read and implement from the get-go. Failure to do so can result in some pretty agonizing consequences.

Take for example the story of Lord & Taylor's "Paisley Dress Campaign." They worked with fifty fashionistas who are Instagram influencers. Each fashionista posted pictures of the dress on their community reaching 11.4 million individual Instagram users and led to 328,000 engagements. This was a great success for the campaign of course, but there was just one problem. The influencers did not disclose that they were paid thousands of dollars each to post a photo of themselves wearing the dress on Instagram and other social media sites.

As a result, the FTC had to take legal action on the retail company. You don't want to find yourself in such a situation so please learn everything you can about laws and regulations before accepting a dollar from any company.

You might be thinking that you're "too small" to get in the crosshairs of the FTC because they only focus on big-money advertisements like a hundred thousand dollar commercials, right?

Wrong. They actually monitor social media just as carefully as any other advertising platforms. I mean yes, social media is massive, and the sheer volume of content is perhaps impossible at this time to monitor each and every single one, but still, you shouldn't try the sneaky approach. It's a huge risk and ethically speaking it's just not right. Better to just adhere to the moral so that as you grow, it becomes part of your standard level of performance online.

The other all-important reason to stay on the right side of the law with your sponsored ads and endorsements is that the more transparent you are with your tribe, the more successful your campaigns will be long-term because you'll never risk losing the trust of your audience. They will know when you're sponsoring a brand and when you're generously sharing unpaid content. This trust is priceless because it leads to that perception of authenticity. If your audience loses confidence in you and thinks you're sneaky or manipulative, it can almost be impossible to gain it back. So set yourself up for success and be open about the brands you work with.

Here are several FTC guidelines to help you get started:

• Sponsored social media posts should include clear disclosures such as "#sponsored," "#paid" or "#ad" before any links leading back to a brand's landing page.

• Endorsers shouldn't talk about their experience with a product or service if they haven't actually tried it, or used it as they say.

• If an endorser is paid to review a product but had a horrible experience, they can't say that it was wonderful.

•In a blog post, the disclosure statement must come before the affiliate link and above the "fold" or "scroll."

•On image-only platforms, disclosure should be over the picture in a clear font that contrasts sharply with the background.

•For videos and audio content, there must be either an audible verbal disclosure at the start or a written declaration on a clearly legible title card at the beginning of the video.

•Make sure influencers don't use tiny fonts or pale colors to disguise sponsorship disclosure.

•Ensure influencers disclose sponsorship as close to the beginning of the content as possible.

I recommend you read through the entire FTC guidelines thoroughly to avoid undesirable situations and clearly and conspicuously disclose the business relationship with a brand whenever you post something.

Chapter 06: Marketing and Advertising

The most effective way to grow a community of super fans and exponentially grow your influencer brand is to learn how to market your brand authentically.

Now, it bears clarifying that marketing and advertising are not one and the same. In case you get confused by these terms, let's do a brief description of each term.

Marketing can be described as the big umbrella that covers every touch point you make with a prospect or client (paying and non-paying). Assistant professor of marketing for the Gabelli School of Business at Roger Williams University, Kathleen Micken defines marketing as everything an organization does to facilitate an exchange between itself, and it's clients.

In your case, your organization is your brand, and your clients are both the companies you want to work with as well as the tribe you nurture.

Advertising is just one piece of your marketing puzzle. It is actually a subset of marketing; an activity that comes with a hard dollar cost attached. When starting out you may or may not include advertising into your marketing plan, but marketing itself is not optional. Unless you know how to market yourself to both types of clients, you don't stand a chance at becoming a highly paid social media influencer.

- The two types of clients you need to serve with excellence
If you want to do well and get paid thousands of dollars each month as an influencer, you must do a good job attracting and serving the two clients that determine how wealthy you can be in your space.

The first type of client is your audience or tribe.
These are your followers or the individuals that form your tribe. The more known, trustworthy and credible you become the more influential and desirable you become to your second type of client. When building your business, your followers are your first clients, and even though they don't spend money on you, their attention is the most important investment they can make with you.

The more you have their attention and influence their behavior, the more money you can hope to make. Why?

Because in the influencer marketing world, money follows attention.
So you want to make sure all your marketing plans are well laid out to ensure that every touch point where your client interacts with you, your content and brand is an experience that keeps him or her captivated.

The second type of client is the potential company or brand that could pay you to partner up with them.
This is where influencer marketing comes into play. And with stats like the ones I am about to share, you should be very thrilled to grow your brand because the potential to earn a wealthy living are virtually unlimited at this point.
• Around 40% of people reported that they purchased a product online after seeing it used by an influencer on YouTube, Twitter or Instagram. Twitter says users now trust social media influencers nearly as much as a friend or neighbor.

• According to a study by Tomson, influencer marketing yields a $6.50 return on investment for every dollar spent.

• When it comes to millennials, 33% of them say they trust blog reviews for their purchases, but only 1% of them believe traditional advertisements.

It's no wonder influencer marketing is becoming a priority for brands. And they are looking for influencers with both large and small followings. Remember the stats I shared about Macro and micro influencers? That's why choosing the side of micro-influencers is a better path to stardom for you especially if you don't have Kardashian money to fund your online activities.

What matters most for businesses interested in influencer marketing is the level of engagement a community has and how pleasant the relationship is between the influencer and the company. After all, if you don't do a great job helping a company reach its objectives, it's unlikely you'll be able to build long-term growth.

Bottom line. Marketing is going to be critical for you at every phase of your business growth, and you'll have to think of it as a two-sided coin. On the one hand, you need a plan that will help you nurture a fantastic audience. On the other hand, you need a program that will help you attract and retain high paying brands.

So far I have been sharing tips to help you attract and nurture an amazing community. Before moving on to section four where we dive deep into each of the platforms so you can set up shop and start implementing all these ideas, let me share tips on how you can market yourself and your brand better so that companies can quickly see the value of working with you.

Tips to marketing yourself and your brand in a noisy and competitive marketplace

• Stop trying to find the "right tactic" or "secret marketing sauce" and instead focus on the core message.
Your "WHY" is the main thing you should be focused on at all times. If you haven't watched Simon Sinek's video on YouTube (start with "Why"), I recommend you do that once you're done reading this.

You'll hear a lot of gurus making a fuss about where you put your call to action button, the color of your buttons on a landing page or the font that you use. And these are all great, however, getting lost in the tactics and logistics of marketing may actually do more harm to your brand as an influencer.

You are in the business of serving people. Focus more on why you want to serve as an influencer in your niche and how you make people feel whenever they interact with your content. Those feelings that your audience feels when interacting with you are what result in actions further down the line.

• Start thinking about this audience you're growing as human beings not a means to an end.
The allure of becoming famous, making a lot of money and living a luxurious life can totally distract you from the significant aspect of wanting to be an influencer in the first place.

Being responsible for a community, for helping people feel like they matter and gaining their trust is a huge deal. You are dealing with human beings, not follower count or leads. Shift from that very limited mindset and start seeing yourself as a steward of something much bigger than yourself and your marketing will sparkle because you'll be creating it from the heart.

• Only do, say, create and advocate for things you honestly feel connected to.
I say this because so many influencers make decisions based on the money they could make. They end up saying and doing things they don't feel connected to which of course flops because their audience also fails to connect and take action.

Your community has the same BS meter that you have, and they know when you're not being genuine about a product or topic. If you're following a script that doesn't feel right for your brand or forcing yourself to follow marketing tricks that gurus have said work, your clients will both pick up on this "fake energy."

Think of all the marketing tools, resources, and tactics as suggestions because in truth no one really knows what will work best for you. Marketing is about testing things out. Anyone who tells you any different is just sabotaging your success.

What works for one influencer in your same niche may not work for you because you are a unique individual and your personality is what makes all the difference in this industry. So blindly following what others say isn't something I recommend. Learn as much as you can and be willing to experiment, but at the end of the day, always follow your gut and what feels right for you and your community.

• Be prepared to go the extra mile
Jay Abraham said in an interview that it's arrogant to think that the market should just come and find you. In other words, he was saying you can't just sit there and wait for your tribe to happen or for brands to show up on your DM with invitations for partnerships.

To build your brand, you must market yourself and your brand. You must work diligently and advocate for yourself. Find ways to be published in relevant magazines and website, do press releases, pitch every brand you can possibly think of and do your best to build relationships with fellow influencers who already have an audience you can add value to. Be extremely active on all the relevant social platforms that you wish to dominate and offer your time to teach, share insights or even create content that can be cross-promoted. Your lack of imagination and creativity is the only limitation here. You can market your brand in so many ways and get in front of new people each and every week, but you must be willing to put in the time and effort.

Without consistent effort in your marketing, you won't become a great marketer. And as a social media influencer, marketing is where you shine. The more you can develop this skill and learn to gain attention even without advertising budgets, the more valuable you become as an influencer. Of course, you can also add in layers of advertising to boost the content you create, increase reach and raise brand awareness for yourself, but these require extra funds and a learning curve that this book doesn't get into.

Marketing is a core component of your success as an influencer, and although I have barely scratched the surface here, you now have enough knowledge to get your brand up and running. It's time to set up shop on the platforms you want to dominate.

Key highlights from this section:

• You need to create a brand identity that resonates with your values as well as the tribe you want to nurture.

• Package your services so that it's easier for your prospects to process information about you, your brand, the type of audience you serve and why they should collaborate with you.

• Use the power of storytelling to stand out and differentiate yourself from the rest of the influencers in your niche. This is one of the most effective ways to connect with your audience, gain their trust and grow your brand.

• At some point on this journey, you will need to start putting together a team. This will require you to prep yourself beforehand and get clear on the culture you wish to cultivate as well as the type of people you want to have working with you. An average team will yield average results; a great team that enjoys working together and supports your mission wholeheartedly will help you exponentially scale your business.

• To stay in the goodwill of your growing tribe, social media platforms, and the FTC, remember to read and follow al influencer marketing guidelines. Maintain transparency and authenticity.

•Marketing and advertising is not one and the same thing. When starting out, advertising may be optional for you, but marketing is a must.

• You must serve your clients with excellence. Your tribe is your client, and so are the brands that pay you to endorse their products and services. They all deserve the best from you.

• Focus more on your "Why" and how you make your clients feel. The emotions that your clients experience when interacting with you are by far the determining factor of whether your brand will thrive and whether you will be positioned as an influencer in your niche.

• You are a steward and nurture of your community. The people that follow you and perceive you as an influencer deserve your care, and you should treat every single person as an essential human being, not a lead or a means to an end.

• If you BS your audience they will feel it and lose faith in you and your brand. As the FTC guidelines put it, if you use something and it wasn't fantastic, don't try to "fake it" just because you're getting paid. The reason your community trusts you and takes on your recommendation is that they believe you will protect them from false claims and direct them towards truth and the things that will actually improve their lives.

• Marketing is a skill set that you can only get better at through practice. Learn as much as you can, test and experiment and enjoy the process of figuring out what works for you and what doesn't. At the end of the day, always go back to your gut and your "why."

• Marketing yourself is a must. And it is hard work that requires consistent effort. So roll up your sleeves and do the work. Stay on your own lane, avoid distractions, keep your priorities straight and expect that soon enough the market place will recognize the value you bring as long as you keep bringing it.

Section Four

" People influence people. Nothing influences people more than a recommendation from a trusted friend. A trusted referral influences people more than the best broadcast message. A trusted friend is the Holy Grail of advertising.
- Mark Zuckerberg

Chapter 07: The Platforms

Now that you have your niche chosen, your business and content strategy ready, it's time to learn more about the social platforms that could make you a superstar. To become a highly paid social media influencer, you need to dominate one or more social channels, and this is the section that helps you choose the best fit for you.

If you want to enjoy a fraction of the influence and followership that people like PewDiePie or Jacksepticeye (self-made YouTubers) experience, then choosing your platform carefully is a must.

My recommendation is to start with one or two social platforms maximum. Strive for depth and mastery within your chosen platform rather than trying to be everywhere. If you try too much too soon and you don't have a team to support your growth you'll just dissipate your energy and resources. And you might not get the necessary traction to grow your tribe.

Brands aren't necessarily looking for an influencer who is big on all channels. Depending on their objectives, they might work with a relatively small influencer who dominates just one channel. So don't get so worked up about building multiple communities all at once. Establish yourself and your tribe on one platform and then expand as your influence grows.

Below I share with you everything you need to know about the leading social platforms where influencers are making money. Since this book is meant to take you from newbie to pro in the shortest timeframe possible, I intend to share as much relevant information about the channel and the subtle differences you need to be aware of as you set up your accounts as well as the different content types that have been proven to work. I even do my best to share some real-world examples of influencers in various niches so that you can get some extra inspiration for your niche. Be sure to customize this information to suit your needs and niche market.

Facebook

This social platform has dominated the world of socializing online. At the time of writing this, there are over 2.23 billion monthly active users globally and growing. Every second there are 20,000 people on Facebook, which means in just 18 minutes there are 11 million users actively using it. Talk about endless opportunity to grow your audience.

Facebook generates $1.4 million in revenue every hour. Most of their income does come from advertising, so when it comes to audience reach and brand awareness, they are certainly demonstrating that it is a pay to play arena.

66% of all millennials (15 - 34-year-olds) use Facebook. 31% of US senior citizens are on Facebook and users spend an average of 21 minutes per day on Facebook.

How to set up your Facebook Fan page:

Step one: Fill out your necessary information and how you want to represent your personal brand.

Go to https://www.facebook.com/pages/creation. Once there you'll see two options - "Business or Brand" and "Community and Public Figure." Choose whichever feels congruent with your objectives and continue following the instructions provided. My suggestion is using the Business or Brand option. In the end, you will have shared some of your information, and the page will start to populate.

Step two: Add a profile photo and cover photo

Facebook will prompt you to upload a profile image and cover photo or video.
The profile image dimensions are - 170 pixels wide by170 pixels tall.
This photo will appear as your icon every time you comment on a post or publish in the news feed. Ideally, you want to upload a good image of yourself rather than a logo.

The cover photo dimension is 820 pixels wide by 462 pixels tall. This appears across the top of your page and is a great opportunity to deliver a visual element that supports your branding, draws in attention and elicits emotion from your visitors.

According to Facebook, your cover image is displayed at different sizes on desktops and on smartphones, i.e., 820 pixels wide by 312 pixels tall on desktops and 640 pixels wide by 360 pixels tall on smartphones so if you want to use a single image that works for both my recommendation in that 820 x 462.

If you are feeling more adventurous try testing out a cover video instead of an image or a feature slideshow of images.

Step three: Finish filling out your information

Facebook will show you a few tips to complete your Facebook Page set up. You'll see a section right in the middle of your new Facebook page where you can click to "See All Page Tips," and it'll walk you through everything you need to do. Be creative about this. It forms part of the copywriting and messaging that represents your brand. All the details you fill in will appear on the About tab of your Facebook Page, and here you can add your origin story, awards, mission, etc.

Before moving on to the next step, I also want you to create a username for your page to make it easier for people to find your page. This will also give you a custom URL that you can share with others.

I also want you to add a prominent call to action by using the button that Facebook provides below the cover photo. It's a great opportunity for your new audience to take the next action and become part of your tribe.

Step Four: Customize your page

Go to Page settings, and you'll find a "Templates and Tabs" tabs. Here you can configure the look and feel of your Page. Tabs are fundamentally different sections of your Page such as your posts, photos, testimonial reviews, etc. You can decide which tabs you want on your Page and their order.

If you are going to have a Facebook Group (which I recommend if you want to be a Facebook Influencer), you can choose the template that allows you to highlight it. You can link it to your Facebook Page for more visibility.

Step Five: Publish your first post

Now it's time to add fresh new content to your new page. This can be a status update, a link, an image, a video, an event or a milestone. Adding content to your page consistently and regularly will make your page look all the more attractive to new visitors as they discover you.

And there you have it, your Facebook Fan Page is up and ready to deliver some amazing content to your new tribe and fans. It's time to start implementing the content strategy you decided on and work on growing that audience.

Most influencers who are active on Facebook also build a community using Facebook groups. But a common question I've gotten is "what's the difference between the two and do I really need one?

It's a tough one to give a simple answer to because both are quite popular. They aren't identical, and I would say, if you want more organic engagement (especially since the new algorithm took effect) it might be worthwhile having both. Let's detail some critical features of each.

Facebook page
• Has built-in analytics (Page Insights).
• Has a call-to-action button (CTA) where you can invite new visitors to Learn More, Sign Up, Book Now, etc. directly from the Facebook Page.
• You can like and comment as your Facebook Page.
• You can add apps and services to your Facebook Page so that your fans can easily order/purchase products, make a booking, get a quote and so on.
• You can boost your Facebook Page, Page posts and Events with Facebook ads.

Facebook Group:

• Has built-in analytics, which is a pretty new feature (Group Insights).

• You can set your Facebook group as exclusive and private (Closed or Secret).

• You can do group chatting with group members.

• Your members always receive notifications about new posts to the Group.

There are some best practices for Facebook posting that you may want to consider. I'll be sharing some of that once we help you set up your group. So let's jump into that.

How to set up your Facebook community:

Facebook groups are the place to connect with other like-minded people, and it's becoming increasingly crucial for a social media influencer to have if they want to cultivate a large community. Follow these steps to create your Facebook Group from within the Facebook Page you just created and start nurturing an engaged community.

Step one. Decide on your Facebook Group Name and privacy settings

All you need to do once you have a name is to click on "Group under the "Create" section at the bottom left sidebar on Facebook. You can also do it directly from your Facebook Page. Fill out the necessary info in the pop-up and hit create.

Step two: Fill out your Facebook Group's info

From your Group settings (you can locate this by clicking on the three-dots button below your cover photo), choose "Edit Group Settings."

• Add a cover photo.

Again, the dimensions I recommend for this is 820 pixels wide by 462 pixels tall. Make sure the photo aligns with your brand.

• Select a group type to help people understand what the group is about. Depending on how you want to position yourself, Facebook gives you several options to choose from.

• Create a descriptive copy to help your tribe understand what the group is about.

You have up to 3,000 characters for your group description so try to be as detailed as possible. And yes, you can use emojis here.

• Add tags to help your tribe find your group.

You can use up to five tags. Think it through and make sure these are keywords that connect your brand to the ideal audience. As you start typing Facebook will offer suggestions.

• Add your location if you want to attract more of a local audience.

By adding a location people who are interested in your topic or looking for a group in your local area will easily find you. You can also add multiple locations if you want.

• Customize your Facebook Group URL.

Use an easy to remember URL so that as you share your Facebook Group on other platforms or in network events and conferences, people will quickly find you. The maximum is 50 characters but the shorter it is, the better.

Step three. Add or invite friends and promote your Facebook Group

Head on over to the "Add Members" field on the right of your Facebook group and start asking more people to join your new Group.

To add a friend you can enter their name in the field, and he or she will automatically join the group without having to accept an invitation. If you want to invite a prospect or new customer just enter their email address. You can also add a personalized note on the invitation by clicking on the tiny blue icon on the right.

To share your new Facebook Group click the "Share" button just below your cover photo. This allows you to share on your timeline, Messenger and Facebook Page. Don't forget to circulate this on other social platforms as well where you're growing fans.

Step Four. Set guidelines and moderate discussions

You can either write them in your group description like some people do or create and pin a post. You could even create a Facebook document. Include things such as the actions that are encouraged and those that should be avoided. Also, let your tribe know who the team members are and the respective roles in case they need support. I also recommend you edit your membership and posting settings so that you can moderate and be in control of all that happens within the Group. Go to "Group Settings" and set permissions for new membership and posting depending on what you feel comfortable with.

If you would like to learn more about new members as they join, you can ask them to fill up a short questionnaire. Ask up to three questions, and they'll have up to 250 characters to share a bit more about themselves.

One of the cool things about the Facebook Group platform is that you or your moderators can remove posts and comments on posts that violate the guidelines. And if you keep getting a member who continuously violates your group you can remove and block them from the Group entirely.

Using Facebook Groups to increase brand equity

Facebook groups are an excellent way for you to generate more engagement around your brand. To cultivate a group that is responsive and engaged, post regularly, have a strategy around the content you share within the group and keep checking the insights to inform your publishing strategy. I also suggest finding creative ways of running things like contests, giveaways and other types of events. In-person meet-ups are also a great way to build a meaningful connection with your community.

Most popular niches on Facebook:

If you're wondering whether your niche market would work well on this platform, here is a small list of some of the best performing niches.

• Fitness

- Dating
- Personal Development
- Make Money Online
- How To's
- Spirituality and Alternative Beliefs
- Sustainability
- Minimalism
- Green Energy
- Survival Niche (DIY)
- Sports
- Parenting
- Camping
- Real Estate
- Religion
- Digital Marketing
- Design
- Photography
- Videography
- Art

Best practices for growing your Facebook following:

1. Make sure your images are at least 180 pixels wide by 180 pixels tall, and the cover photo is 820 pixels wide by 312 pixels tall.

2. Leverage the power of Facebook Live. It's the best way to interact with viewers in real-time. Your followers will receive notifications whenever you go live so they'll know to tune in to receive your broadcast at just the right time.

3. The best time to post of Facebook according to collected research done by Coschedule on both mobile devices and desktop computers depends mostly on the type of audience you serve. No single answer fits everyone. So here are three slots to test out. 9:00 AM, when people are just going online for the first time or about to start working. 11:00 AM - 12:00 PM when people

are taking their lunch break. 3:00 PM - 4:00 PM especially if you're growing your brand around software and education. The best days to post on Facebook are Thursday to Sunday.

4. Test out the different types of media content to see which one your tribe engages with the most on this channel. A video, single images, multiple images, blog posts with URL, native posts are all worth testing out until you find what works, then keep creating more of the same.

5. Listen and improve as you create and publish content on this platform. The feedback you get from your followers should inform you of the direction the brand needs to take. Learn from your tribe and improve your brand as you engage directly with all your followers.

Instagram

At the time of writing this, Instagram has over 1 Billion monthly active users and is the second most engaged network after Facebook. 60% of its users log in daily, and the most significant demographic is aged between 18 - 24 years.

Although most of Instagram active users are under 35 years old, it still carries a substantial demographic that most brands want to target. It's no wonder most social media influencers want to be known on Instagram. The rewards of having a powerful tribe on Instagram can be very gratifying.

Some influencers claim to charge upwards of $25,000 for a single Instagram post. Influence Central found that consumers actually rank Instagram influencers sixth place on their level of effectiveness when it comes to influencing purchases. It's definitely not an exaggeration to say your riches could be sitting on Instagram as we speak!

Now that you already have your niche picked out and a content strategy ready to deploy, it's time to set up a noteworthy account.

How to set up your Instagram

Instagram is mobile only, so you've got my permission at this point to get out your phone while reading this to follow along. Your phone needs to be Apple iOS, Android, Windows 8 or later. As long as it's not an old Nokia or Motorola (do they still make those?), you'll be good to go.

Head over to the App store (specific to your phone type) and search for Instagram App. It's a free download that should begin instantly. Once you have it installed, it's time to sign up.

Sign up

Use a relevant business email that matches all your other social media profiles if possible. That way you'll have all notifications in one place. It's also important to keep your usernames and brand name as uniform as you can across all platforms. So the Facebook account you just created should match or be very similar to this Instagram page and any other social profile you create.

Your biography

This is where you set up your profile picture. Make sure it's recognizable, crisp, clear and free from clutter. You can decide whether to use a logo instead, but just I recommended on your Facebook Fan page, using your image is better for building an influencer brand. In fact, if you can use the same image across all social platforms, it will be even better.

The recommended profile picture size is a square image of 110 pixels wide by 110 pixels tall.

Next, you have limited characters to share a little about yourself, what you do and your brand. You can add your tagline or brand slogan here, and with a bit of creativity, you can do both if a few sentences. Check out other influencers in your niche market for some inspiration.

The other important thing to add on your bio is a link, which can be added from the "Settings" tab. You only get one link across the whole platform so choose wisely. Of course, you can change it as often as you like but always make sure this link drives traffic to an important landing page or website at all times.

Turn it into a business account

By default, you begin with a personal profile. To use Instagram for business, you have to connect your account to a Facebook Business Page (the one you just created above). Inside your Facebook Page settings on the left side, you should see the Instagram icon at the bottom. Click on it, and you'll be prompted to connect the two accounts and even switch from a personal to a business account. Just follow the instructions, click confirm, and you're all set. Now you can be able to view more detailed insights and analytics of your audience behavior and content performance.

Publish visually appealing content

It's time to start adding images and videos to your Instagram gallery. But in Instagram aesthetics are everything! You cannot be an Instagram influencer without a carefully crafted visually attractive theme. Your photos in the feed should good and represent your brand accurately from the color palette, font, photo arrangement, etc.

Many Instagram influencers identify and follow a specific style of editing their photos to ensure the color is uniform. Tools like VSCO or Lightroom can be a great asset to help you edit your photos. I also know influencers who create epic content using the in-built filters in Instagram so don't feel like you have to make things so complicated but do make sure you don't compromise on quality.

Once you know how to use Instagram for business, you can create Instagram stories to drive engagement and expand your reach.

What are Instagram stories?

These are short videos or photo collections that disappear after 24 hours. At the time of writing this, they are probably the biggest trend on Instagram with more than 200million Instagram users using Instagram stories daily. It's an effective way to share entertaining heartwarming moments with your followers. You can also get the attention of people who aren't following by adding relevant hashtags or locations.

Most popular niches on Instagram:

If you're wondering whether your niche market would work well on this platform, here is a small list of some of the best performing niches.
• Fitness
• Luxury/ Lifestyle
• Animals
• Travel
• Fashion

- Beauty and Makeup
- Business/entrepreneurship
- Relationships
- Design
- Making money online
- Art

Best practices for growing your Instagram following:

1. Choose hashtags that will enable your content to be found by other Instagram users. When choosing your hashtags, don't always strive for volume. Just because a lot of people visit a specific hashtag doesn't mean they are ideal for your tribe. You want to aim as close as possible to your ideal audience.

2. Post consistently. Most influencers post daily and some even multiple times a day. You must create a schedule for yourself that allows you to regularly put out fresh content so that your audience can get accustomed to receiving communication from you. Studies done reveal that an increase in posting frequency can boost engagement rates. This doesn't mean creating unrealistic schedules for yourself. Be mindful of how you plan out your time, and if you need some help, you can always use tools like Buffer to help you create and publish content in advance.

3. The best times to post on Instagram across industries are 1:00 PM and 5:00 PM, i.e., during lunch break and at the end of the typical workday. The best day to post on Instagram is Friday.

4. Make sure the size of your Instagram images is 1080 pixels wide by 1080 pixels tall. Your Instagram stories should be 1080 pixels wide by 1920 pixels tall, and the maximum file size is 4GB.

5. To succeed in this social platform as an influencer, build a brand that's centered on selling a lifestyle rather than a product. Be inspirational, motivational and inclusive with your copy and speak to both your paying and non-paying clients. If you can find a way to provide your very

own splash of unique energy and charisma and create a vivid feed, it will go a long way in establishing what your brand stands for and who it caters to.

6. Cross-promote your dedicated hashtag to all your other profiles. You can also print it in your print ads, receipts, and other offline activities.

7. Be more active locally. See what's going on in your local neighborhood or a city you're targeting. You can do this by going on the search page and choosing the "Places Tab," then type in the name of the place to see all geotagged posts for that location.

8. Block out some time daily to go through accounts in your niche and "like and comment" other people's photos. You can find relevant users by going through the hashtags you usually use or view the followers of your favorite Instagrammers. Start with 5-10 photos on each person's account to get their attention. Make sure you leave a genuine comment and give them a follow if they resonate.

9. Geotag your photos so that other people who used the same geotag can see your picture and potentially follow you since you now have so much in common.

10. Approach popular users and ask for collaboration. This requires some creative thinking and a generous heart. For example, ask another Instagrammer in your niche if you can "take over their account" for the day as a guest contributor. Instagram story takeovers are a great way to grow your following dramatically, and they can be loads of fun. Test them out!

11. Encourage more User-Generated Content (UGC). By encouraging your growing audience to participate in your journey either through contests, giveaways, etc., and offering something they would want, your audience is more likely to share pictures of themselves with your product. With a little creativity, you can come up with a great giveaway that doesn't cost you much but generates lots of engagement, sharing, tagging and promotion of your brand organically.

Twitter

Twitter has 313 million monthly active users. It's most known as the go-to platform for customers to discuss brands. This makes it very appealing for a social media influencer who wants to attract an audience of buying customers.

To be an important influencer on this platform, you need to understand the dynamics of Twitter conversations and what your role should be as an influencer.

The most powerful type of Twitter influencer you can become is known as a hub influencer. According to an in-depth study of Twitter conversations done by the Pew Research Group and the Social Media Research Foundation hub influencers are the key people at the center of their conversational networks. These are the people creating virality by starting movements, creating hashtags and population the trending board. A hub is usually an influential individual or a media organization.

As the center of a conversational network your role as a hub influencer would be to tweet new information to a vast network of followers, then those followers retweet that information.

Becoming a hub as an individual isn't easy. You must consistently produce original information that is noteworthy enough to warrant retweets. You also need to have enough of the right kind of followers to gain retweets.

This takes us back to all the exercises we've done in section one and two of this book. Helping to prepare you, honing down your niche and understand how to attract your ideal audience. Without a definite niche and a tribe, your content (regardless of how fantastic it is) would go nowhere.

Another type of influencer you could become on Twitter is known as a bridge influencer. The difference between being a hub and a bridge influencer is that as a hub influencer you create viral movements and hashtags whereas as a bridge influencer you connect related groups and create virality by sharing relatable content from one group to another. In other words, as a bridge influencer, you don't have to produce information because your primary role is to publicize it. Your influence comes from your positioning. You connect the thoughts and ideas of one group to another and identify relevant points among groups to serve as a channel for that information.

The best and quickest way to become a bridge influencer is to connect with the "hubs" in your niche as well as in niches that have an effect on your primary niche. One of the critical aspects of succeeding as a bridge influencer is being able to understand the conversational structure in which you exist. What do I mean by this?

For example, if you're in a Polarized Crowed (Pew research study defines it as two large dense groups of people that talk about the same subject but do not connect to each other or use the same words), then realize these people don't really interact with other groups. As such you can serve as a link between the polarized network and outside conversations. As you can see, a lot of strategy goes into becoming a Twitter influencer. It has to be very intentional and well planned if you want this to work but once you position yourself either as a hub or bridge you're far more likely to become recognized as a Twitter influencer and consequently reap the rewards.

Before sharing some best practices for both types of Twitter influencers, let's talk about the setup process.

How to set up your Twitter account:

Step one. Your profile name

Head over to the Twitter website and click sign up. One of the first things you'll have to decide is your profile name. This becomes the name or twitter handle you'll have also known as @name.

I recommend using your real name or the name you're using to establish your brand. If you can use the same name as your Facebook Fan page, Instagram account, and Twitter, you create a congruency that helps build your credibility. You'll also want to make the account user your full name as well, and please keep your @name short and memorable otherwise no one will remember it.

Step two. Add a photo of yourself

Please avoid using a logo as much as people. You are a social media influencer. Your personality and relatability will help build up your brand quicker, which means the more people see your face, the better. This image is displayed any time you post a tweet, so you want to differentiate yourself from everyone else in the Twitter ocean. And if you use the same image on Instagram and Facebook, it becomes easier for your followers to spot you on this platform as well. The best recommendation for image size is 400 pixels wide by 400 pixels tall even though it only displays 200 x 200.

Step three. Your twitter bio

Just as with Instagram, you have a limited character bio (160 characters). This is your chance to tell everyone what you do, why you do it and what you're passionate about. Make it exciting and friendly so people can feel comfortable making a connection with you. There are many times I've read a bio and decided to follow that person purely because of how they expressed who they are and what they stand for.

Step four. Add your website or a landing page

Twitter gives you a little section to add your website, any social platform you choose or another landing page. Even if you don't yet have a site utilize this spot to drive people to your Instagram account, Facebook Group or Fan page. If you have a blog or an "about me" page, this is also a great link to use.

Step five. Add a header background Image

A lot of people forget to do this, but as an influencer, that background image is super important. It's your chance to engage your audience and make them curious about you using something visual. This is often the first thing your visitors will see so make it captivating.

The best recommendation for image size is 1,500 pixels wide by 500 pixels tall.

Step six. Follow relevant people

Look at people in your industry that interest you, other influencers that you want to start connecting with and hubs that you want to start learning from. Don't just follow celebrities.

Now that you've followed a few people, it's time to publish your first tweet. The only way to learn and get good at tweeting is to test and experiment. At first, it will seem like you're just talking to the wind, but if you keep at it and build connections with the right people; you'll soon be part of conversations that can build your following. Don't forget to keep an eye on who is talking to you and about you. By regularly checking your "mentions" you'll be able to speak to the right people, respond to those reaching out and establishing yourself as relatable.

Most popular niches on Twitter:

If you're wondering whether your niche market would work well on this platform, here is a small list of some of the best performing niches.
• Celebrity News
• Gaming
• World News
• Sports
• Health and Wellness
• Tech
• Politics
• Travel
• Personal Development
•Digital Marketing

Best practices for growing your Twitter following:

1. Get very niched right from the start and discern the type of information you want to either create or share that will best serve your niche.

2. Do your best to remain relevant and on topic especially on this platform because it's such a fast-paced platform that makes it super easy to be ignored.

3. When starting out on Twitter (especially if you choose to be a hub influencer), you should follow the most significant people in your network. In fact, I recommend connecting to "bridge influencers" so you can quickly become familiar with the subtle nuances of your niche, the best hashtags, vocabulary to use, etc.

4. Work on building bonds and connections within your chosen niche. These connections are the ones that will help you build momentum and an engaged audience.

5. Be super responsive on Twitter. You must thank those you retweet and reply to your tweets. And please avoid twitter wars at all costs as it only messes with your credibility. Twitter is mainly about making connections and building dialogue so if you want to succeed on the platform align with the nature of the game.

6. The best time to tweet on average is around 8:00 AM - 10:00 AM as well as 6:00 PM - 9:00 PM. If you are in the B2C space, then you can the recommendation is that you post more on weekends while if you are targeting a B2B audience, then weekday tweets will probably work best for you. If you also want to maximize retweets and clickthroughs then aim for noon or 5:00 PM - 6:00 PM.

YouTube

As with every other channel we've talked about so far, this powerful channel (although harder to conquer nowadays) can serve your mission of becoming a highly paid influencer as long as you understand who your audience is and what they want. Video content is perhaps the fastest way to grow your brand and get the attention of your tribe as well as other brands.

YouTube is the second most visited website in existence according to Alexa.

On average, people spend eight minutes and forty-one seconds each day on YouTube. 1.9 billion logged-in users are visiting YouTube every month in 2019. That's literally half the Internet.

Cisco predicts that video will be 82% of all Internet traffic by 2022.

96% of 18 - 24-year-old American Internet users use YouTube, and 85% of 45 - 54-year-olds are using YouTube so if you're worried about reaching your target age group, trust me, everyone can be reached. YouTube has better numbers when it comes to older age groups than Facebook.

The top ten YouTube stars earned 42% more money in 2018 than in previous years meaning; the demand for influencers continues to grow. Forbes estimates that these ten men earned a combined total of $180.5 million in 2018. There's no denying the potential for non-traditional marketing with macro or micro-influencers is expanding, and it's not too late for you to grab your piece of the pie.

How to set up your YouTube Channel:

Step One. To set up a YouTube channel, you need a Google account

So first, head over to Google and create your account if you haven't done so already. Once you have the account, you can easily find the YouTube icon by clicking on the navigation menu on the right corner of your Gmail.

Step Two. Sign in to YouTube and click on the user icon at the top right of the screen

You should be able to see a gear icon that will lead you into your account's "YouTube Settings." Click on "Create a new Channel," decide on the name (again I recommend following the same as the other social platforms to create brand congruency). Add your brand name and click create.

Step Three. Fill in the "About" section

This is where you will fill out your profile and channel description. Here you should describe your brand and what viewers can expect to see on your channel. This is also where you can add links to the other social media networks as well as your website. Please keep in mind that this description will appear in more than one place on your channel so be thoughtful, implement some of the copy that you came up with for your brand messaging and elevator pitch.

Step Four. Upload a cover photo for your channel

The first thing visitors see when they come to your YouTube channel is the cover photo so use this to introduce people to your brand. Give them a visual experience of what you have to offer as a brand and a person. The more aligned this cover photo is with your brand style, messaging as well as the other cover photos used on Twitter, Facebook and other social networks the more enhanced their perception will be about you.

The recommended dimension for your cover photo is 2560 pixels wide by 1440 pixels tall with a maximum file size of 4MB.

Step Five. Publish your video content

It's time to start making some magic with your video content. Assuming you have implemented everything we discussed earlier in the book, you are now fully equipped to produce world-class content. And no, you don't need fancy equipment or a big production team to publish videos that your audience will love. If you own a smartphone and an earpiece you are ready to produce amazing videos. As long as you know who you're targeting and what message you want to share, hit the record button, speak to the camera, edit it, upload it and publish.

Test out different types of videos relevant to the niche market you are serving and be sure to add in lots of inspirational content as well. Having variety in your video content is a great way to start testing what resonates most with your growing audience.

Step Six. Optimize for video search and Google search

Your video ranks on Google as well as YouTube search, did you know that?
To make sure it's optimized for ranking fill in the title, description and tags sections when uploading a video. These are essential if you want your video to be easily discoverable so don't overlook this part. Have a keyword strategy in place and optimize every video for the Keywords you want to rank for. Given the fact that YouTube is a Google-owned product, by implementing some SEO on your videos you'll find yourself ranking on both search engines.

Step Seven. Create a channel Trailer

Create an amazing introduction using a channel trailer and make sure you grab the attention of your new visitor within the first 5 - 10 seconds.
This trailer is usually a short and sweet video that introduces your new visitor to your channel. It's a great way to welcome the visitor and let him or her know who you are, what your brand is all about and what kind of content they can expect to see in the future.

Step Eight. Integrate your channel with your website and social media networks

If you have a website, you can add a YouTube widget to help drive website visitors to your channel. YouTube also allows you to connect your associated site to your channel which helps a lot with search results and also as a form of verification that your website is the official brand owner of the channel.

You can also start sharing the content you create to all your other social platforms. A good trick that I like to use is creating shorter "teaser videos" for my Instagram and encouraging people to go watch the full video on YouTube. It seems to work very well on Instagram and is worth testing on Twitter as well.

Step Nine. Engage with your growing audience

As with all social platforms, interaction and engagement is everything. You must build a community around your channel. Reply to comments, ask and answer questions and more importantly, listen to your people and what they have to say. Your viewers watch your content and share their insights because they are interested in you. Give them more of what they want, and you'll have a very active community. Gary Vaynerchuck is an excellent example of how powerful YouTube can be if you are continually creating interactive and engaging content.

Most popular niches on YouTube:

If you're wondering whether your niche market would work well on this platform, here is a small list of some of the best performing niches.

• Tech Videos.

• Gaming

• Food

• Fashion

• Beauty

• Travel

• Animals

• Comedy/ Humor

• Product Reviews

• How To's

Best practices for growing your YouTube community:

1. Invest enough time coming up with creative and engaging intros for your videos. You only have less than ten seconds to grab someone's attention and get him or her hooked to your channel so make it count right from the get-go.

2. Develop emotional sharpness and find fresh ways of expressing this in your videos. Your video has to be moving. It has to make you laugh, cry, ponder profound questions, learn something you didn't know, think in a certain way and engage your curiosity. It should also be sharp enough to evoke a specific reaction from your audience. They should either decide to love your work or hate it. You don't want to be an in-betweener! This is where we get back to the earlier exercises we did in this book where we determined how we want your audience to feel when interacting with your content. Focus on how you want them to feel rather than executing a perfect script.

3. Be different in your niche. Use your brand to express your own unique voice. If you do your research well, you'll be able to know what's missing in your niche and what other influencers in your niche are doing that's working, and also that's not working. By knowing what "the crowd" is doing, you now have a springboard from which to create your unique concept offering something fresh that does ultimately help you stand out. All this is possible if you do your research well.

4. Use branded thumbnails in your videos. Make sure your YouTube channel stands out and becomes easily recognizable by adding some cool customized thumbnails to your videos.

5. Always have a visible "Subscribe" call to action in every published video. You can use annotations where relevant or just add something that aligns with your branding style as you're editing the video so that it blends in seamlessly with your content.

6. Promote your videos on your other social platforms. Share your videos on Facebook, Twitter, LinkedIn, Pinterest, Scoop.it, and any other relevant platform.

7. Shoot in HD or higher quality and make sure the audio quality is excellent. Nothing will turn off your audience faster than a video that of poor quality and poor audio. This is super important, so please invest in the right equipment.

8. Use YouTube cards to reduce abandonment and boost engagement. The longer someone stays on your channel, the longer they are active on YouTube (so YouTube rewards users who can hold the attention of the audience). Using your video analytics, you can be able to see the exact point people tend to lose interest and abandon your video, and then you can place YouTube cards at that point to hold their attention and potentially get them to click on other videos.

9. Add a sub confirmation to all your YouTube links. This is a low hanging fruit that many influencers fail to utilize. You can implement on your other social media channels as well as your website. All you need to do is to use the sub_confirmation link when sharing the link to your YouTube channel (instead of just using the regular link). When a user clicks on this sub_confirmation link, the first thing they'll see on the YouTube is a popup asking them to subscribe to your channel. Go ahead, add it on now and watch as more subscribers start showing up as you go about sharing your videos.

Chapter 08: Taking your brand from unknown to influential

Going from zero influence on social media to building a personal brand that's well known with thousands (even millions) of followers is not that complicated. Anyone can do it, but few do because the hard part is the daily grind that goes into building up the momentum. Overnight success is real. It just takes years of preparation and momentum building before that tipping point occurs. To be fair, not all influencers are overnight successes.

Take for example two YouTubers in different niche markets. One girl (a videographer) went from 3,000 subscribers to 150,000 subscribers within a two-week time frame. The reason for this "overnight success" was the fact that she had been creating fantastic content for more than 2 years and built an active community around her brand. And at some point, she decided to create an exclusive video for a famous artist that she admired and asked her community members to share and circulate the video and tag the artist so that he could see this video inspired by him. Her community shared it all across Twitter, and the buzz created a big enough wave to get his attention, which led to him retweeting and commenting. Of course, the YouTuber's reach expanded and within two weeks she exponentially exploded her growth and got a chance to communicate and offer her services to the artist. Overnight success? Of course. But it was two years in the making!

There's another girl I want to tell you about. She's the YouTuber building a brand in the beauty and makeup niche. Her current following is at 450,000 subscribers and she's made it all from scratch since she was in high school. She now does campaigns with brands like Avon and for a young girl barely in her mid-twenties, she's earning an excellent income. Her success did not experience any sudden spikes. She slowly built the brand one subscriber at a time over the years. It was her patience, passion for her topic and amazing content that has continued to build momentum to the point where brands were willing to give her pitch a try.

So you see dear influencer, the road to your fame and riches is not set in stone. There is also no shortcut to it. The time it takes to become famous is unknown but what is certain is that if you

180

stay on your path and do the work without compromise or loss of enthusiasm, discipline, and passion, you will win.

To go from known to influential, you must be consistent. And I don't just mean publishing your content once a week, I suggest doing it for years. The people that end up creating influential brands are those that stick with it long term. You also need to experiment with various media types. That means podcasting, video, blogging, etc. Your tribe will most likely have different desires on the type of content they want to consume. The more you can satiate their different preferences by appealing to their tastes, the more you'll draw them in. This doesn't mean you need to produce different content for video, podcasting and written material. It means you need to get creative and include a repurposing plan within your current content strategy.

Another essential fact to reiterate here is that you must genuinely care about your audience. Again this goes back to the exercises we did in section one of this book. If you don't know why you're doing this and if you don't really feel that people should believe in you and have confidence in your ideas because you genuinely care about serving them in a certain way, then it's going to be tough becoming a social media influencer.

Social media is about socializing and exchanging ideas. It's about caring for each other and listening to each other. You need to become that person that helps others out, the reliable, caring, trustworthy virtual friend. That's not something you can fake. So if you genuinely do care about your people and feel you are the right person for your topic then keep forging your path because you are bound to receive the great harvest of online influence.

With that influence comes the added benefit of having brands write you a check just for being you and doing your thing. Not too bad right?

Well, before you get all excited about that check, it's important I mention that it won't just fall out of the sky. If you really want to earn some good money, there are some things you need to get right. Let's address that next.

The pitch the pricing structure and charging what you're worth

If you are serious about becoming a social media influencer by any means, then I certainly recommend taking the time to work on your mindset as well as the pitch you make to companies, sponsors, editors and more. I have learned over the years that there are definite ways you can help your prospects receive communications from you with an open mind.

Due to the novelty of our industry, brands, and business owners are still very skeptical about dealing with influencers or getting into influencer marketing because they worry about getting ripped off, shafted or slandered online. They also struggle with understanding how to measure the ROI of their investments. Knowing this, I am dedicating some space to share tips about how you can craft the perfect pitch once you are ready to take the plunge.

Before sharing the tips, however, I need to call out the elephant in the room. Why? Because it's perhaps the biggest obstacle to an influencer's financial success. You can be great at nurturing a community and building a brand, but if you have mindset blocks around selling, you'll continue to be broke. It will be hard to close deals with other companies and making an offer to your audience will feel incongruent and ultimately lead to little action from your wide audience. To help you with that, you need to work on your current mindset around money and selling.

You must charge what you are worth, not too much and indeed not too little. Since it's still pretty much the wild wild west when it comes to pricing for influencer marketing, I encourage you to find price points for your services that enable you to deliver excellent value for excellent pay. And reiterating what I said before if the mindset is an issue, you better work on those money blocks!

Now, let's talk about how to craft the perfect pitch:

Tip One. Use a warm, friendly but professional tone

Your tone really matters when giving a pitch. In influencer marketing, it's not about being overly formal and pretentious. Be yourself, use the same tone that you portray on your brand so that as businesses check out your work, it will feel congruent. It is possible to be casual friendly and professional at the same time. I find this works best.

Tip Two. Find a specific contact and name

Unless it's just utterly impossible to send a personalized email to a specific contact, I recommend doing your research and getting hold of one particular person. This tactic usually warrants a quicker response.

Tip Three. Gain insights on your audience demographics

Getting to know who is in your tribe is super important. You might discover there is a slight variation in demographics as you move from one platform to another. Having this information will help you know how to serve best your community, which brands to work with and what products/services will be more appealing to the various platforms you dominate.

This is the first crucial step before pitching any brand because as a general rule, your audience will want to know things like where your audience lives, average age group, gender, etc. The valuable insights you offer to a brand during the pitch process, the more you can negotiate and demonstrate expertise.

Tip Four. Make sure you do your homework on the brand

Never approach a brand unless you feel confident you already understand enough about their marketing, how they like to communicate with their target audience and the value you see yourself bringing to the table that further enhances whatever they are currently doing. Think of this pitch from their point of view; not yours.

Ideally, you want to be able to show businesses that by working with you they will reach their objective or even surpass it. Some research questions to get your juices flowing are - What channels are they active across? Are you already doing any influencer marketing campaigns? Who is their target market? What products are you interested in promoting the most?

Tip Five. Explain what you do in no more than 2 sentences and describe yourself in 5 words or less

Yes, you read me right! You need to keep that intro as short and sharp as possible. Don't write too much when approaching a cold lead. People are so busy nowadays and have very low attention spans so if you don't keep the entire pitch brief, and to the point, you'll probably lose their interest and never get a response.

When describing yourself, use a distinctive title or phrase that will cause the reader to think, "hmm, that sounds interesting" or "I'd like to hear more." When explaining what you offer always make the brand feel that your offer is equivalent or higher in value than what you're asking for. This is called the 51/49 strategy, i.e., give more than expected.

An example template:

Hey [insert name]

I hope your week is off to a great start! My name is Kendra, I'm an influencer, and I write the Canadian-based blog, [insert website], you can see some of my recent posts here. In the last year, I've grown my IG following to over 19k highly engaged followers. I'm reaching out because I'm currently in planning mode for the 3rd quarter in which I'll be working on quite a few fitness posts. In particular, I've been dying to try out [X fitness brand] high-performance compression tights and would be interested in doing a review on my site (typically valued at $300). My 12,000 weekly readers have been asking for a Q&A post on fitness products so I thought this would make for a great organic partnership! Is that something you'd be open to? Please let me know your thoughts - would love to team up on this!

Side note. I consider a rejection a response too. By receiving an answer back (whether it's an answer you like or not), gives you an opportunity to learn, get feedback and see where to improve.

Tip Six. Know your worth

As I mentioned before, you need to be able to charge what you're worth. If you don't know your value, even your pitch won't come across strong and genuine enough. Earning money as an influencer means you must be good at influencing - both paying and non-paying clients.

The more data and insights you have about your community engagement, who they are and how responsive they are to you, the easier it will be to pitch with confidence because you'll have proof of the monetary value you want in exchange for your efforts. Show the brands specifics about your "influence" to help the brand increase their confidence in you and then, price yourself accordingly.

In summary, the critical aspects to a great pitch once you've done your homework and feel ready to start pitching small and large companies is to:

1. Describe and show the brand why you are the best micro or macro influencer to work with.

2. Talk about your fantastic audience and let them know specifics about demographics etc.

3. Lay out your offer and detail why it would make sense from their point of view as a brand to invest in your fees.

4. Use evidence to back up your offer. Include your stats, case studies, analytics, and more data!

Chapter 09: The Eleven step formula if you're just getting started

Always think big and start small. Baby steps taken sequentially and consistently will ultimately take you to the top of the mountain.

Step 1: Do a self-audit and get your mindset right.

Have a point of view. Know yourself really well. Why should your tribe listen to you? Why should people follow you? Figure out who you are at the deepest core and what your mission is. What's your polarizing point of view that will definitely not please everybody but will totally attract the right people to you?

Step 2: Pick a niche.

Today you might have one or zero followers; one day you may have 200,000 followers. How you get there fast is by starting out as the expert among your friends and peers. Then work toward being the expert in your city and state. Lastly, launch your global empire. It starts with just one vertical, following that thread into mastery and then expanding from there. This is what a niche will enable you to accomplish, and that's why you need to complete all the practical exercises in section one and two to hone down what your niche will be, what your passionate about and what your brand style will be to embody and compliment that chosen subject matter.

Step 3: Identify and define your ideal audience.

Take the time to hone down your ideal audience so you can build a tribe that positions you as a person of influence. The best way to do this is by getting into the mind of your ideal audience. You must do empathy mapping and really understand who they are, what they care about, where they are hanging out online and what motivates them.

Equipped with this knowledge you can now create content and a brand that is worthy of being followed. People today want to find meaning in the brands they follow. It's your job to show them why they should be supporting and having faith in your ideas.

Step 4: Create a content strategy and marketing plan

Once you have a niche and know the tribe you're marketing to, it's time to build out your strategy. Dive deep into the marketing and content strategy outline provided in this book. Be sure to experiment with a variety of media content, plan for repurposing strategies and any advertising if applicable to you.

Step 5: Select your channels

Whichever platform you choose to start with, learn as much as you can about it. Because each social network hosts varying users, the channel you select will require its own strategy. And when you expand to a new channel, you'll have to create a totally different strategy. Take the information shared in section four and let it guide your approach to growing organically the type of audience you wish to serve.

Step 6: Network within the Industry

To be influential, you need to make real connections both online and offline. Sitting at home on your couch will not get you results. Get out in the world and attend major events related to your niche. Venture outside of social media and participate in real life conversations and gatherings so you can enhance your reputation, influence, and connections.

Step 7: Engage with your community

I encourage you to be very proactive when it comes to responding to your tribe. But don't stop there. Start conversations, ask questions, create debates, etc. The more you can engage with the community the further you will spread your influence. This includes even outside your own feed. Post in groups, tag other influencers and respond to interesting conversations that other influencers have started.

Step 8: Consistently publish fresh world-class content

After devoting an entire chapter on content creation, suffice it to say the quality of content you produce will determine your quality of success as a creative influencer on social media. This will be the foundation that elevates or destroys your brand perception so make sure you give it everything you've got.

Step 9: Quantify your efforts with data

Make sure you're tracking, measuring and collecting all your data as you grow. Each social site shows you insights that help you understand your audience better, the performance of your content as well as paid ads campaigns. Use this to your advantage. Keep a record of everything especially as you start growing because these stats, analytics, case studies and other types of data will become invaluable when you're ready to pitch to companies looking to get into influencer marketing.

Step 10: Collaborate and reach out to influencers in your space

To quickly become an influencer, you'll need to know and hang out with a few influencers yourself. Who you are following is almost as important as who follows you. Reaching out to other influencers is an excellent way for you to get exposure and share your message in the marketplace in ways you otherwise wouldn't be able to on your own. Just make sure you do this from a place of "giving" rather than "getting."

Step 11: Reach out to paying brands and start monetizing your brand

At this point, you started from scratch with nothing, and you now have influencer friends, a growing tribe of loyal fans and data that can help you back up your influencer pitch to paying brands. It's not time to advocate for your brand and reach out to the right companies that are either already doing influencer marketing or want to do influencer marketing.

Never sit and wait for an opportunity to come knocking. If you feel it's time to start promoting and monetizing your brand, then it is time. Grab your tools and media kit, compose that perfect pitch and start teaming up with brands that are dying to see better results with their marketing. Don't forget to use the customizable template that I shared with you when you start reaching out to companies. And by all means, shoot for the stars!

The next step on your influencer journey

Now that you have found your unique identity on social media and you know how to set yourself up for success as an influencer, it's time to start implementing the plan. Be consistent, stick to your strategy until you gain some traction. You've now found your little corner on social media to grow yourself and build a brand an audience that helps you live out your mission.

Persist on this path of becoming an authority figure in your niche and master just one platform at a time (whether that'll be Facebook, YouTube or Instagram first), to massively improve your chances of exponential success. Focus on depth and concentrate your energy on one vertical rather than trying to be everywhere all at once. This is how you'll take your business to the next level where scaling up becomes the natural consequence.

By implementing everything, I've outlined in this book, you will naturally stand out from the crowd and sooner rather than later, other brands will start to notice you. That's when the money will start pouring in. But you can't keep your eyes on the money; stay focused on doing your thing and serving your tribe. Each and every platform discussed has the potential to make you very wealthy as an influencer, and I assume by now, you have at least set up your accounts following the step-by-step guidance I gave you. Within your grasp is the chance to become an influencer and change lives (including your own), but you must be willing to put in the work.

Overnight success doesn't come to those who just sit and wait. You might have no followers at the moment, but as you keep adding value to the marketplace and mastering your craft, you'll start growing your followers faster than you could have imagined. This is a world that rewards action so whatever you do next, make sure it is activity geared toward the realization of your dreams. And lastly, remember, no one really cares unless you can help with something they care about. Now go out there and gain some influence!

Recommended Resources:

Want to learn even more about taking your already established brand to the next level? Here are some additional resources that I have found useful.

Influencer: Building your personal brand in the age of social media - https://www.amazon.com/Influencer-Building-Personal-Brand-Social/dp/0806538856

The rise of social influencers: A new age of digital marketing - http://blog.influence.co/rise-of-social-influencers/

www.ingramcontent.com/pod-product-compliance
Lightning Source LLC
Chambersburg PA
CBHW051754200326
41597CB00025B/4550